"This is an excellent book. It offers sound advice to parents and to grandparents. Seasoned parents will learn from it. And, it will be indispensable to those who are shepherding their first child through school."

—Robert M. McClure, Co-director,
NEA Charter Schools Initiative

"Clear and timely for parents, this book not only addresses some of the feelings children may have about school but also acknowledges some of the mixed emotions that parents experience."

—Linda A. Braun, Executive Director,
Families First Parenting Program

"If you've ever wondered what goes on in your child's life away from home, at that mysterious edifice known as school, you're in luck. Ann LaForge has written the book for you."

—Lawrence Balter, Ph.D., Professor of
Applied Psychology at New York University

"This is a special combination of reassurance for parents in these challenging times and solid advice on how to help every child succeed."

—Dorothy Rich, Founder/President of
The Home and School Institute,
and author of *Mega Skills*®:
*Building Children's Achievement
for the Information Age.*

What Really
Happens in
School

What Really Happens in School

A Guide to Your Child's Emotional, Social,
and Intellectual Development, Grades K–5

Ann E. LaForge

HYPERION

NEW YORK

To Christopher
Vivamus atque amemus

Copyright © 1999 Ann E. LaForge

Library of Congress Cataloging-in-Publication Data
LaForge, Ann E.
   What really happens in school : a guide to your child's emotional, social, and intellectual development, grades K–5 / Ann E. LaForge.— 1st ed.
      p.   cm.
   Includes bibliographical references (p.291).
   ISBN 0-7868-8211-5
   1. School children—United States—Psychology—Handbooks, manuals, etc.   2. Child development—United States—Handbooks, manuals, etc.   3. Education, Elementary—Parent participation—United States —Handbooks, manuals, etc.   4. Home and School—United States— Handbooks, manuals, etc.   I. Title.
   LB1117.L22   1999
   372.18—dc21   98–43988
                                                                        CIP

First Edition
10 9 8 7 6 5 4 3 2

Design by Interrobang Design Studio

Table of Contents

*W*hen my first son started kindergarten (back in 1994), I had every intention of being an "involved" parent. I had written enough articles on education by then to know how important parent involvement is. And I knew that hundreds of studies had shown that with *any* child it can make a positive difference in grades, behavior, attendance, and self-esteem.

And, of course, I wanted the best for my child. But what I didn't realize back then is how tricky staying involved—or even just *informed*—can be.

Times have changed considerably since my own mother packed me a snack, gave me a kiss, and sent me off to school. And the challenges today are many. I've learned the hard way, for example, that:

- *It takes time to stay involved.* And time is one commodity most of us parents have in short supply. Between the morning rush to get everyone off to school and work, and the evening crush of feeding, bathing, soothing, and playing, it's tough to find a moment to even talk about school. Add more than one child, plus homework and after-school activities to the equation, and you often end up with barely enough time to cover the daily routine.

- *There are no set standards.* Like it or not, our country has no formal national curriculum. Each state is empowered to set policies, guidelines, and minimum standards for its own school districts. And different school districts enjoy varying levels of autonomy.

    Even within the same school, when there's more than one classroom per grade, not all kindergartners do the same activities, and not all third graders read the same books. So it's not always easy to know what to expect your child to be studying, or whether or not she's getting the best education possible.

- *You can't rely on your child.* I learned that on my son's first day of school, when I picked him up. "Well, how was it?" I asked with excitement in my voice.

    "How was what?" he asked back.

    "School!" I said. "How was school? What did you do in school today?"

    "Oh. Nothing," he replied.

    "Nothing?" I asked, perplexed.

    "Nothing," he said.

    "Didn't you read any books, or sing any songs, or make any new friends?" I persisted.

    "I don't remember," he said. "Can I watch TV when we get home?"

    It was a classic conversation. And one that's oft repeated. In fact, nearly anyone who's ever sent a child to school has had it—and felt frustrated. As one mother puts it, "I know I'm supposed to be an 'involved' parent, but it's hard to be involved when my son won't even tell me what he did at school all day!"

- *You can't rely on your memory.* For one thing, it's probably blurrier than you think. For another, it may not serve you all that well in understanding what and how your child is learning.

The focus of elementary school education has shifted since we parents were in school (and it's still shifting). New theories about how children learn and what they should know have led to changes in everything from the teaching techniques to the classroom terrain.

Teachers now view themselves more as facilitators than lecturers, for example. Instead of feeding their students information to memorize, they're teaching them how to formulate questions, find answers, and evaluate different solutions on their own.

And students are playing a more active role in their own education. Instead of sitting in nice, straight rows and listening to the teacher or pushing pencils across worksheets, they now often work in groups, on hands-on activities that look more like play than schoolwork. They may spend their time in various "learning centers" throughout the classroom, and they often learn important lessons while sitting in a circle on the classroom floor.

In addition, students today often read real children's literature, instead of just prepackaged reading texts, and they're allowed to invent spellings for words they don't know how to write. During math periods, instead of just memorizing their basic facts, they fiddle around with blocks, or cubes, or little plastic teddy bears to build their understanding of mathematical concepts.

Add to all this the influx of new technology—such

as computers with CD-ROM capability, interactive video systems, educational television programs, educational software, and access to the Internet—and you can count on being confused. As one father of twins told me, "When it comes to school, I feel like a third wheel. So much has changed since I was a kid that I can't help wondering what—or whether—my children are really learning."

GREATER ROADBLOCKS

On top of all this, children are growing up more quickly these days, and elementary schools are being forced to deal with problems—like domestic violence, gun use, and drug abuse—that were practically invisible in schools a decade ago. As a result, there are lots of subjects being taught in school that we parents never studied—such as conflict resolution; multicultural appreciation; ethics; values; career education; environmental studies; healthy living; drug, cigarette, and alcohol avoidance; and even safe sex.

In addition, to keep up with all the information kids today need to learn (and to make life a little easier for working parents), many school systems are experimenting with longer school days, a longer school year, or a year-round school calendar.

So you can't just take it for granted that your child will have the same kind of learning experiences at school that you did. Nor should you necessarily want that. Thanks to technology and other changes, the world our children are growing into will be quite different from the one we exist in. They'll need different kinds of skills (a comfort with technology, for instance, and the ability to manage information, solve problems, and work cooperatively with people from diverse backgrounds) in order to succeed as adults.

THE IMPORTANCE OF INVOLVEMENT

While all of these challenges make it harder than ever to stay involved in a child's education, they also make it more important than ever to stay on top of what's happening in school. That's where our children do most of their learning, growing, and socializing from kindergarten through twelfth grade. And it's mainly where they develop their sense of personal abilities and accomplishments, and set their goals for the future.

So what's a busy parent to do? I've been asking that question of other parents, teachers, principals, school psychologists, and education experts for more than eight years now, and I find that most of them say the same thing. To be an "involved" parent—and to give your child his or her best chance at success—you have to:

1. *Make the commitment.* Your child's success at school has to be important enough for you to *want* to find the time and the energy to stay on top of what's happening in the classroom. That may mean giving up work time to occasionally volunteer to help in the classroom or chaperone a field trip. It may mean staying up half an hour later, to make sure you read through all of the papers—notes, newsletters, homework assignments, permission slips, and book orders—that your child brings home in her backpack. Or it may mean waking up earlier than you'd like to make sure your child gets her homework done, eats a good breakfast, and gets to school

on time—with all of the materials the teacher requested. It'll probably feel like thankless work, but it should yield wonderful results.

2. *Become informed.* Understanding the new teaching goals and techniques will help you support what your child learns in the classroom. And learning what's normal—both socially and academically—for children at different grade levels will make it easier for you to:

   - find out what your child has learned—and needs to learn
   - evaluate the teacher's curriculum
   - expand learning outside the classroom
   - communicate and work with the teacher when your child is having difficulties
   - understand and solve school-related problems
   - foster friendships and build your child's social skills
   - motivate your child to do—and be—the best he or she can.

HOW THIS BOOK CAN HELP

Step number 1 is up to you. But this book can help with Step number 2. Each chapter focuses on a different grade, from kindergarten through fifth, and offers an inside look at what goes on at that grade level in most classrooms.

Because of the diversity inherent in our educational system, this book can't give you an exact picture of what your individual child will experience during any given school year. But it will help you understand how children at each grade level *tend* to behave. It'll also provide important insights into what the key subjects are, how they're taught, how much homework to expect, and how to handle peer pressure.

You'll also find a full section (chapter 7) devoted to explaining the ten most important things you can do to help your child succeed in school at any grade, as well as a chapter (8) that answers common questions about giftedness, learning disabilities, and resistance to going to school.

The information in each chapter comes mainly from extensive interviews with more than forty experienced classroom teachers from all parts of the country and a variety of educational settings, including public, private, and parochial schools. (For a complete list of participants, please see the acknowledgments on page xvii.)

With an average of fifteen to twenty years' experience under their belts, these teachers have seen the educational process develop; they've watched teaching trends come and go; and they've dealt directly with countless children from diverse backgrounds, with a broad range of behaviors and abilities. They know better than anyone what life is like behind those closed classroom doors. And they know firsthand what children need most in order to succeed in school.

I also interviewed parents, principals, school psychologists, and other experts, to round out the grade-by-grade profiles.

READING THIS BOOK

You probably won't read this entire book in one sitting. Instead, I hope you'll keep it handy on your bookshelf, so you can consult it as each new school year begins.

Though you might be tempted to read only about the grade your child is going into, it's a good idea to also read (or skim) the chapters before and after that grade level. In the elementary school years, there is a great deal of overlap and uneven development—among both the children and the curriculums. In any given classroom, there may be students who are one or two years apart in age, for example, and four to five years apart in development. And with any individual child, physical, emotional, social, and cognitive development may be at very different levels at any one time. So material that's introduced during one school year must often be reintroduced and reinforced the next. Plus, teachers use and reuse many of the same strategies.

Also, the tips and advice offered in any one chapter (such as how to ease the transition during a new school year or how to help with conflict resolution) will often be useful for children at other grade levels as well.

My overall goal with this book is to give you what I always felt I needed as my first son began his formal education: a general map of the territory. That way you can tell where your child is supposed to be heading, and help him discover the best way to go.

Acknowledgments

*T*his book would not have been possible without the generosity and support of many different people. In particular, I'd like to acknowledge and thank the wonderful, dedicated teachers and other school professionals who stuck with me through lengthy interviews and provided a wealth of information and insights. I'm especially grateful to:

CHRISTOPHER AGEEB of Colbert Elementary School in Hollywood, Florida.

HELENE BLACKMAN of Eagle Elementary School in West Bloomfield, Michigan.

GEORGE BURNS, Middle School Head at the Bank Street School for Children in New York City.

SHARI CUTLER of Wapping Elementary School in South Windsor, Connecticut.

NANCY Y. EVANS, director of primary education at Lake Ridge Academy in North Ridgeville, Ohio.

JULIE FERRISS of Madison Avenue Elementary School in Madison, Mississippi.

JOHN H. FUNK, an early childhood specialist with the Granite School District in Salt Lake City, Utah.

KAREN GEIGER of Amy Beverland Elementary School in Indianapolis, Indiana.

LINDA R. GRAF of The Community House School in Forest Hills, New York.

RAE ANN GREMEL of Philip R. Smith School in South Windsor, Connecticut.

KAREN GUNTHER of The Kew-Forest School in Forest Hills, New York.

KATHY HOEKENGA of Trinity School in Menlo Park, California.

DONNA HUPE of Haine Middle School in Cranberry Township, Pennyslvania.

SUSAN M. JAMESON of Boyertown Elementary School in Boyertown, Pennsylvania.

MARCIA A. KENYON of Eastwood Elementary School in West Fargo, North Dakota.

ELLEN O'ROURKE KNUDSON of Victor Solheim Elementary School in Bismarck, North Dakota.

JEAN LAGRONE of Westside Community Schools and Westgate Elementary School in Omaha, Nebraska.

STEVEN LEVY of the Bowman School in Lexington, Massachusetts.

THOMAS R. LEWIS of Jane Addams Elementary School in Moline, Illinois.

MICHELE MANOS of The Kew-Forest School in Forest Hills, New York.

DEBBIE MARSHALL of the Duke School for Children in Durham, North Carolina.

BARBARA MAUGHMER of Amanda Arnold Elementary School in Manhattan, Kansas.

DEBBIE MAXA of Philip R. Smith Elementary School in South Windsor, Connecticut.

ROBERT M. McCLURE, co-director of the National Education Association's Charter Schools Initiative.

JILL MERMELSTEIN of Glenallan Elementary School in Silver Spring, Maryland.

LORI MURAKAMI, an assessment specialist with the San Francisco Unified School District in San Francisco, California.

CYNDY NOVOTNY of Woods Learning Center in Casper, Wyoming.

ELIZABETH PERKINS of Arcanum Elementary School in Arcanum, Ohio.

CATHY PIHL of Kate Bond Elementary School in Memphis, Tennessee.

KATHY A. PRIDDY, curriculum coordinator for the Mineral Springs Elementary School in Winston-Salem, North Carolina.

CHERYL REARDON, a basic skills coordinator at Constable Elementary School in South Brunswick, New Jersey.

KIMBERLY C. REICHERT of The Kew-Forest School in Forest Hills, New York.

MARGOT SAWICKI of Public School 101 in Forest Hills, New York.

SANDI SCHMIDT of Lake Ridge Academy in North Ridgeville, Ohio.

CHARLOTTE SCHUMACHER, a reading primary specialist at Lake Ridge Academy in North Ridgeville, Ohio.

FRANCES B. SERGI of The Kew-Forest School in Forest Hills, New York.

MARGIE SHEA of Lake Ridge Academy in North Ridgeville, Ohio.

JUDY A. SHELDON of Booker T. Washington Elementary School in Dover, Delaware.

EDWARD J. SILVER of Millington Elementary School in Millington, Maryland.

CONSUELLO SMITH, a reading specialist for the Westfield Public Schools in Westfield, Massachusetts.

SHARON SMITH of Dry Creek School in the Rio Linda Union School District, in California.

TULIP TITUS of Woods Learning Center in Casper, Wyoming.

CINDY WAMPLER of Boyertown Elementary School in Boyertown, Pennsylvania.

DORIS WILLMANN of Lake Ridge Academy in North Ridgeville, Ohio.

I am also extremely grateful to the people who put me in touch with the wonderful teachers I interviewed, and contributed invaluable insights during informal conversations. My special thanks go to:

SUSAN WHITMORE of the communications department at the National Education Association.

PHILIP V. ROGERS, Jr., headmaster, MARGARET MACCARY, assistant headmaster, and *all* of the teachers, students, and staff at The Kew-Forest School in Forest Hills, New York, who did everything they could to help with this book (that includes you, Sara and John).

JIM WHITEMAN, head of the lower school at Lake Ridge Academy in North Ridgeville, Ohio, and all of the lower school teachers there who welcomed me into their classrooms.

MARGARET MASON, curriculum and staff development director at the Duke School for Children in Durham, North Carolina, and all of the excellent teachers there who taught my son Gus.

KENNETH JOSEPH, principal of Public School 101 in Forest Hills, New York, and his dedicated teachers and staff.

KAREN JOHNSON, a certified speech/language pathologist with the South Windsor Public School System in Connecticut (and my sister).

DOROTHY RICH, president of the Home and School Institute and author of *MegaSkills®: Building Children's Achievement for the Information Age*.

BARBARA WILLER, director of public affairs for the National Association for the Education of Young Children.

I owe an enormous debt of gratitude to the many wise parents who were willing to share their school experiences. Thank you so much: Pam Allen, Anne Arjani, Judy Bloom, Denise Bullwinkel, Chris Burton, Daniel Cunningham, Carolyn Davenport, Tamara Eberlein, Catherine Gilfether, Beth Gillespie, Ronnie Hochberg, Holly Hughes, Charles James, Ronald Kern, Becky Laurin, Joan Lenowitz, Mary Mitchell, Thomas Mitchell, Jane Blake Murray, Katy Musolino, Terri Palma, Julie

Ritzer Ross, Peggy Schmidt, Janet S. Schwartz, Sally Vesty, and Elizabeth Young.

I'd also like to express my sincere gratitude to:

TONI GERBER HOPE, for giving me the back-to-school assignment (for *Redbook* magazine) that eventually became this book;

LESLIE WELLS, of Hyperion, who not only made this book happen, but showed considerable patience as it was being written, and a keen eye for editing when it was done; and

PEGGY SCHMIDT, of New Century Communications, for not only acting as my agent, but for offering insightful comments on the manuscript and—more importantly—for being there when I really needed both an advisor and a friend.

Last but not least, I offer love and thanks to all of the family members and friends who encouraged me through this project and many, many others. Thank you, especially Norine, for your support—and for the loan of the Pink House. Thank you Tommy, for being such a generous brother. Thank you Mom and Dad, Margaret, Dan, Kevin, Ellen, and Gay, for your special help. And kisses galore for my sweetest loves: Christopher, Gus, and Teddy.

As soon as he turned four and a half, my younger son, Teddy, began asking about kindergarten. Somewhere, somehow, someone had told him that "real school" begins when you're five and go to the "big kids' school." So all he wanted to know was: "When is my birthday?"; "Will I be five on my birthday?"; "Will I go to kindergarten on my birthday?"; and "Is kindergarten fun or hard?"

He acted as though he could hardly wait for kindergarten to begin. But he also sounded anxious. "Will my friends be there?" he wondered. "Will the teacher be nice? Will I still have time to play?"

Clearly, his emotions were mixed. But not nearly as much as mine. Part of me was excited about this big step in his life. It meant the two of us had survived so much. The sleepless nights, endless diapering, potty training, and tantrums of his earliest years were behind us now. And the "easier" years of childhood were ahead.

But I was also unexpectedly sad and somewhat reluctant to let my little guy go. As Mary Mitchell, a mother of three, puts it: "*I* felt more separation anxiety when my son went to kindergarten than *he* did."

"There's something about this milestone that makes you suddenly realize just how fast the baby and toddler years have gone by," Mitchell says. "And even if you're glad they're over, it can be difficult to accept that your little 'baby' will never be a baby again. Children really change once they go to kindergarten," she adds.

LET THE CHANGES BEGIN

In many ways, Mitchell is right. Kindergarten does coincide with a lot of physical and cognitive changes in children. But most of them are positive and necessary. And some of them—such as greater self-reliance and improved self-control—are downright refreshing.

So even if you're feeling uncertain about this milestone, or you're sad to see the "baby" years end, both you and your child have a lot to look forward to when kindergarten begins.

Getting Ready to Go

Making the leap from preschool (or just being home with Mom or Dad) to "real school" can be intimidating. All your child is hearing is how lucky he is to be going to "real school." But all he's thinking is, "Oh, no! I have to go to this new place, with an adult I don't know, and hang out with all those kids who are strangers!"

Fortunately, there are some easy ways to turn that thinking around. Here's how:

- *Attend all of the orientation activities provided by your school.* The biggest issue for most children is fear of the unknown. That's why most kindergartens today offer incoming students a chance to tour the school, visit the classroom, and meet the teacher before school begins. Some even arrange sample school days and trial bus rides to give kids a taste of what's to come.

- *If your school doesn't have an orientation program, create your own.* Over the summer, take your child to the school, peek into the classroom, and explore the corridors, so he's not overwhelmed on the first day. Practice walking from the front door to his classroom, and show him the lunchroom, the gym, the playground, and even the bathroom. If the school is closed, check out the playground.

  Also, make shopping for school supplies and clothes feel like a special occasion, to build your child's enthusiasm.

- *Find your child a friend.* There's nothing more comforting than a familiar face on the first day of school. So if your child has a kindergarten orientation and meets someone he likes, get them together for a play date or two over the summer. If you don't know anyone in your child's class, look for a child in the neighborhood who'll be on the same bus, or at least at the same school. Even meeting a slightly older child who knows the ropes can ease your kindergartner's fears.

- *Talk—and listen.* You don't want to scare your child by harping on how different kindergarten will be. But casual conversations about what he can expect and an open invitation for him to ask you anything will help. Also, check out your local library or bookstore for books about starting kindergarten, and share them with your child.

- *Practice basic skills.* The summer before school starts, help her practice little things like getting dressed by herself; using the bathroom independently; opening and closing her lunch box and backpack; opening and closing sandwich bags, drinks, and other food containers; carrying a tray of food (if she'll be eating in a cafeteria); and even getting on and off a bus. She'll need those skills when school starts.

A Painless-Looking Good-bye

When it comes to the first day of school, you should shoot for a tear-free good-bye. For example:

- *Put your best face forward.* No matter how you're actually feeling, act positive and excited in front of your child. If you seem upset or keep saying things like "I'm going to miss you *so much!*" or "Are you sure you're going to be okay?" your child will start thinking kindergarten is something he should worry about—and then he'll start crying.

- *Be matter-of-fact.* It's okay to tell your child you'll miss her, but say it in a positive way: "I know you're going to miss me, and I'm going to miss you, too. But

I'm so excited about all the fun you'll be having in school. And don't forget, I'll be right here waiting to pick you up when school's over. Then you and I can go home and have a snack, and talk about our days!" Give your child a picture of you or a favorite stuffed animal to put in her cubby and look at when she feels lonely.

- *Watch your body language.* Even when you know the right words to say, you might still give off negative physical cues, such as furrowing your brow, looking sad or worried, or clinging to your child. Kids pick up on these things, so it's best to hide your emotions and save your tears until after your child enters the classroom.

- *Trust the teacher.* If your child is crying and the teacher reassures you that it's okay to leave, do so without a fuss. Experienced teachers have seen scores of children go through the separation process; they know firsthand that most children stop crying soon after the parent leaves the scene. A clean break may seem more painful, but it's usually better for the child.

What Kindergarten Kids Are Like

Every child is unique, of course. But there are many traits that children entering kindergarten (around age five) tend to share. Like preschoolers, for instance, they're often active, loud, dramatic, curious, enthusiastic, and egocentric. They love to tell you what they're doing and ask you how they've done. And they're very straightforward about their feelings. They'll get loud and excited when they're happy, for example, or cry and throw tantrums when they're mad.

But they can do more, say more, and get along better than most preschoolers. By kindergarten, most children have managed separation to some degree. They've also had more experience in the world beyond their homes. Their communication and social skills are better, their attention spans are longer, and their physical abilities are far more refined.

And even though they're still fairly self-centered, most kindergarten kids genuinely want to be good and to please the adults around them. In school, for instance, if the teacher casually observes that there are a lot of toys on the floor, half the class will jump up to help clean the mess.

Always Asking

At home they ask permission a lot—especially when they know the answer is yes (as in: "Can I leave the table to go to the bathroom?" or "Can I have an apple for a snack?"). And they love to solicit compliments. You hear a lot of questions like "I did a good job, didn't I?" and "Am I behaving?" from kindergarten kids.

Actually, you hear a lot of other questions, too. Ask any parent who's been there: "The questions multiply, and they definitely get harder," says Elizabeth Young. "Once, my daughter, Allison, was begging me to have another baby, so she could have a sister to play with. I told her I'd think about it. Then she asked, 'Mom, if you have another baby, can I breast-feed it?' I was so surprised by the question, I didn't know what to say. I finally mumbled something about breast-feeding being the mommy's job. But she kept pressing me with more questions like 'But why? I'm a girl too' and 'What are breasts, anyway? And how do you make them grow?'"

Although conversations like that one can drive an adult crazy, they point to one of the most wonderful characteristics of kindergarten kids: their burning desire to learn. Once you spark their interest in something, they'll do almost anything to find out more.

Not Quite Perfect

That's not to say kindergarten kids are perfect. They're still very young and just learning to control their impulses. They have a lot of enthusiasm and energy (especially first thing in the morning), and they're extremely talkative (sometimes to the point of being annoying). They even tend to think out loud. So at school, when they're really enjoying an activity or lesson, things can get crazy in the classroom. They'll forget to wait their turn, they won't want to share, and they'll interrupt the teacher—not because they're being bad, but because they're so excited about what they're doing.

Even at home you'll frequently hear "Look what I can do..." and "You know what else...?" When a kindergarten kid has something to say, he tries to say it right away, so he won't forget. Plus, kids this age just assume that everyone wants to hear about everything they do and think.

Another trying trait is their tendency to shift from one mood to another, with little or no warning. The child who's being sweet and helpful one minute may be whiny and demanding the next. Like preschool children, kindergarten kids want what they want when they want it. Most of them are used to one-on-one attention and haven't yet developed a lot of patience and impulse control.

Why Consistency Counts

As the year goes by and kindergarten kids begin to feel more secure in their new school environment, they start to test their limits. If the teacher says everyone has to stand behind a certain line, for instance, at least one child will inch his toe over that line—just to see what'll happen. "You really have to follow through on discipline or the kids will walk all over you," notes one teacher.

The same holds true at home. By the middle of the school year, you may discover that you can't get your kindergartner to go to bed on time anymore or to sit quietly and listen to a story. You may even catch him lying, cheating, or stealing. But all of these are perfectly normal behaviors for children approaching age six, and the best way to deal with them is to be consistent with discipline. What works in the classroom—setting fair limits and sticking to them—will also work at home.

What Kindergarten Kids Should Know

"My biggest question, when my first son, Kevin, was starting kindergarten, was: 'Is he ready?'" says Cathy Gilfether, a mother of three. "Because of his summer birthday, I knew he'd be younger than a lot of his class-mates, and I knew he was a shy, reserved child to begin with, so I was concerned. But no matter who I asked, I couldn't get a clear sense from the school about what was expected."

That isn't surprising. While some schools do have kindergarten "readiness" tests, most have the attitude that any child who is five years old by the school district's cutoff date is "ready." Even if there is testing, the goal is usually not to see who's "smart" or "slow," but to get a baseline measurement for each child, so the teacher can tailor activities and lessons appropriately.

"Children enter kindergarten with a wide range of abilities and maturity levels," says Shari Cutler, a teacher at Wapping Elementary School in South Windsor, Connecticut. "Some have been to preschool; others haven't. Some can already read; others don't know the alphabet. A good teacher will approach each child from wherever he or she is on the first day of school."

Teachers' Wish List

Though they don't require it, many teachers like to see children enter kindergarten with the ability to:

- recognize the letters of the alphabet, as well as some numbers
- hold a pencil, crayon, or marker correctly (that is, angled between their thumb and forefinger instead of in a tightly gripped fist)
- work comfortably with scissors, glue, paint, and other art materials
- print their first name (preferably using uppercase and lowercase letters)
- count up to five objects
- distinguish differences in size, shape, and quantity
- speak in complete sentences
- tell you their full name, address, phone number, and birthday
- play by themselves, or focus on one activity with a friend, for up to ten minutes at a time.

If your child can do all of these things—or more—that's

great. He'll be starting school with a lot of potential for
success. However, if he can do only some of the tasks on
this list, or can't do *any* of them, don't panic—and don't
try to launch a crash course in academics to help him
catch up. He won't necessarily have a harder time in
kindergarten than the kid who knows everything.

Real Signs of Readiness

According to teachers, social and emotional readiness are
much better indicators of kindergarten success than academic achievement. So the most important questions are:

- *Can your child separate from you easily?* Many children will cling or cry a little when you drop them off
  on the first few days of school. That's nothing to worry
  about. Usually, as soon as the parent disappears, the
  crying stops and the child starts enjoying whatever's
  happening at school. But if the clinging and crying
  continue, they can affect the child's ability to participate in classroom activities.

  That's why most teachers look at separation skills
  very carefully during kindergarten orientations. If
  they notice that a child is not interacting with others,
  seems frightened about leaving her parent's side, or
  cries excessively when the parent leaves the room,
  they'll usually express concern. A child like this,
  teachers say, might be better off attending a part-time
  prekindergarten program, or simply joining a less
  structured play group, where she can gradually build
  her separation skills.

- *Is he on the road toward independence?* In particular:
  Can he go to the bathroom by himself and remember to

wash his hands and flush? Can he put on his own clothes and manage zippers, buttons, and snaps with little or no assistance? Can he open and close his backpack and lunch box? Can he open the food and drink containers in his lunch box? Can he express how he feels and ask for what he needs (as in: "I don't understand" or "I need to go to the bathroom")? Can he sit quietly and attend to one activity (doing a puzzle, for example, or looking at a book) for ten to fifteen minutes on his own? Can he carry out simple verbal directions (such as "Hang up your coat"; "Put away your lunch box"; and "Come sit in a circle with the other children")?

These behaviors are important for a couple of reasons. One is they affect how classroom time is spent. If a teacher has to help twenty or so children take out their lunches, tie their shoes, and put on their jackets, there's not going to be much time left over for teaching.

But even more important is that kindergarten is more structured than preschool. A child can't just go off to play with the blocks if he has a writing or math assignment to complete. He has to be able to follow directions, move from one activity to another when the teacher says to (not when he *feels* like it), and work at least part of the time on his own.

A child who's not ready to be independent—who still needs lots of help with daily routines, for example, or who can't sit quietly and focus on one project for a brief period—may have trouble adjusting to the kindergarten routine.

- *How does she interact with her peers?* Your child doesn't have to be the most popular kid in her preschool class or already have a best friend in order to do well in kindergarten. But she should at least be interested in playing with children her own age and be able to control her impulses enough to cooperate and compromise with her peers.

These kinds of skills are crucial in kindergarten because they pave the way for learning. Again, children who don't feel comfortable in large groups, who are too shy to take risks in the classroom, or who aren't all that interested in engaging with their peers may be better off attending a half-day kindergarten or other part-time program that allows them additional time to develop those skills.

What "Not Ready" Means

If a teacher or other school professional suggests that your child delay kindergarten or opt for a half-day program don't get too upset. It doesn't necessarily mean that your child is any less intelligent, or less likely to succeed, than her peers. It merely indicates that her developmental timetable is working at its own pace.

According to the latest research, all children follow a predictable sequence of development (in the physical, emotional, social, and cognitive realms) during their first nine years of life. But each child moves through this sequence at his or her own rate. At any given moment, a child might be fairly advanced in one area (say, cognitive development) and a little behind in another (say, social development). But over time, under normal circumstances, development evens out.

So some children—even if they're academically bright—just need a little more time and experience to develop their social skills. This is not something you can force. But it is an important consideration, especially if your child is on the younger side of five when the school year begins.

What to Expect in the Classroom

Some things at your child's school—like the size of the chairs and the smell in the hallways—will trigger an instant flashback to when you were in grade school. But you should also notice some very interesting changes.

"Kindergarten today is totally different—and much better—than what I remember," says Tamara Eberlein, a mother of three. "My kindergarten teacher was very strict and kind of scary looking, and I hated the fact that we were forced to take naps. So I didn't expect too much. But the first time I walked into my son Jack's classroom I thought, 'Wow. This looks like fun!'"

The Fun Approach

Eberlein's reaction is the kind of response many kinder-garten teachers today are trying to elicit—not from par-ents, but from students. Early childhood educators no longer believe that all of the children in a classroom are ready to learn the same thing, at the same time, in a rote way. Instead, research shows that young children learn most effectively when they're allowed to move around, make lots of choices, and use all of their physical senses to explore, experiment, and create.

So nowadays, you rarely see children sitting in their chairs reciting their A-B-C's and 1-2-3's. Instead, the focus is on real-life, hands-on learning. For example, rather than have students color in a worksheet featuring the letter P (the old way), a teacher today might have them "write" the letter P on a cut-out pig, using glitter, dried beans, and beads, or shape the letter P from pretzel dough (and then bake and eat it). Instead of having them labor over a math ditto (the old way), the teacher might teach them a counting song or have each child take a handful of M&Ms and then sort and graph them by color.

The New Classroom

You can usually sense that things have changed just by looking around the classroom. Though no two kindergarten rooms are exactly alike—even when in the same school, right next door to each other—most share a number of elements that encourage independence and educational play. These include:

- small chairs and tables, which are frequently rearranged to suit different classroom needs

- a variety of learning "centers," each of which focuses on a different theme—such as writing, art, music, math, blocks, dramatic play, cooking, or science—and is filled with toys, tools, and other related objects

- a separate reading corner, often featuring a comfortable chair or couch where children can snuggle up with a good book (one classroom I visited had an old-fashioned bathtub filled with pillows; others had rocking chairs or reading lofts)

- lots of different forms of print, from labels on various classroom objects ("chair," "table," "blocks") to books, posters, and elaborate signs proclaiming each child's name

- lots of examples of the students' writing (even if the printing is uneven and the spelling is way off)

- computers stocked with educational games that reinforce basic math and reading skills

- a special carpeted area, where children can gather as a group to share experiences, brainstorm ideas, and plan out the daily schedule

- personalized "cubby" areas that provide each child with a special, private space for storing a jacket, backpack, and other personal belongings

- a lot more movement, talking, and interaction than one would expect in school.

Looks Like Preschool

If your child's kindergarten classroom reminds you a lot of her preschool room—that's a good sign. If the teacher is covering a lot of the same themes (dinosaurs, animals, or space, for example) and using similar hands-on materials (sand, blocks, paint, crayons, clay, and dress-up clothes), that's even better. It doesn't mean your child will be bored. It means she'll probably be learning in the way that young children learn best: by touching, exploring, and discovering.

The difference is that in kindergarten your child will take everything to a new height. Instead of just stacking the blocks in the building center, for instance, he might build an elaborate town and then write (or dictate) a story about how that town was attacked one day by pirates.

Open-ended Action

A key element of the hands-on approach is the open-ended activity: an assignment that has no right or wrong answers. "No two children learn in exactly the same way or at the same rate," explains John Funk, a teacher and early childhood specialist with the Granite School District in Salt Lake City, Utah. "So the goal, today, is to create activities that children at different levels of development can enjoy and learn from."

For example, the assignment might be: "Go to the writing center and create a book about dinosaurs." The child who is not yet reading and writing could go to that center (which might consist of a table stocked with paper, pencils, dinosaur stickers, glue, markers, and a stapler) and produce a book with lots of illustrations. The teacher might then ask the child to dictate his dinosaur story, and write the words for him in his book. As she does so, she can reinforce for him the connection between spoken words and written sentences.

Another child in the same class, who is beginning to write on his own, might produce a dinosaur book using his own words and pictures; the teacher could then spend time with that child reviewing some of the finer points of spelling and punctuation.

Their end products would look very different. But both children would learn from the experience and walk away with a feeling of success.

Integrated Themes

Yet another significant element in many of today's classrooms is the "integrated" or "interdisciplinary" approach. Instead of teaching subjects like reading, writing, and math at distinct times of day (to develop isolated skills), a teacher will work all of them into open-ended activities that support a specific theme and enhance growth and learning at many levels. The themes are carefully chosen to reflect the interests of the children in the classroom, and many teachers encourage their students to suggest themes for the class to study.

For example, when my son Gus was in kindergarten, at the Duke School for Children in Durham, North Carolina, his teacher, Debbie Marshall, introduced a "Nighttime" theme, which evolved into a unit on "Space." To strengthen a variety of skills using the "Space" theme, Marshall had the children:

- read books about stars, constellations, planets, and space travel (*for reading and science*)

- keep individual logs of their observations of the night sky (*science and writing*)

- create "moonscapes" out of scrap materials, to hang on the bulletin boards (*art and fine motor skills*)

- stuff and sew felt pillows shaped like stars and planets, to hang from the ceiling of the classroom (*science, art, and fine motor skills*)

- decorate a huge cardboard spaceship and create space

props for imaginary space voyages (*art, dramatic play, and social skills*)

- build homemade rockets, launch them from a soda bottle, and then measure and graph the distance they traveled (*science, art, math, and writing*)

- follow a recipe to make "moon cakes" (pancakes), and then cook them—carefully watching for "craters" before flipping them over (*math, science, and reading*).

While certain activities (such as reading) involved the entire class at the same time, most days saw small groups of children working on different projects in different centers throughout the classroom. To crown the unit on "Space," Marshall invited the children to gather at the school for a pizza party one night and then accompany her on a walk through the woods near the school, to observe the nighttime sky.

A Hidden Structure

It's easy to be deceived by an academic program like Marshall's unit on "Space," because it looks like the kids are just having fun. But they're learning a great deal in the process.

If you remember sitting at a desk, reciting the alphabet or coloring in worksheets in kindergarten, you may feel uncomfortable when you see your child "playing," as opposed to "learning." However, all of the play activities your child enjoys in school will have an academic focus and a distinct purpose. In fact, kindergarten teaching strategies are much more structured today than they were forty years ago, because teachers now know more about how children develop.

The most important thing to remember is that, for children, play is work. It's how they learn.

The Most Important Subject This Year

If you're thinking it's reading, writing, or arithmetic, you're wrong. Though all of those subjects *are* taught in kindergarten (and all are important), the main focus of this school year is socialization. At this point, children are going to school mainly to learn *how* to go to school—and how to get along in a group.

In most classrooms, the teachers start at ground zero. They focus on everything from how to line up and walk down the hallway, to how to sit quietly in a group and listen while others are talking.

Other important lessons include how to:
- take turns, share materials, and work in small groups
- pay attention and follow directions
- stay in one place and focus on one activity for ten to fifteen minutes at a time
- use words—instead of hands and feet—to express anger and frustration
- remember and follow rules
- make friends and get along with others.

Group Living

The first few weeks of school are usually devoted to teaching and reinforcing the daily routines, such as: what to do when you first arrive; where to put your coat and lunch box; what to do when you finish an assignment; how to get ready for recess and lunch; and where to put things when it's cleanup time so the next person will know where to find them.

There's also a lot of turn-taking and sharing activity. For example, in most kindergarten classrooms, each day begins with a group gathering (known as circle time, team time, or meeting time, for example). All of the children sit on the floor in a semicircle around the teacher and take turns talking, sharing work, brainstorming ideas, choosing activities, and answering questions. There may even be some version of that old classic, show-and-tell.

During the day, many of the assigned activities require two or more children to work together to solve a problem, complete a task, or create a story or piece of artwork. Often, the whole class will participate in writing a book or creating a mural. These kinds of activities help bond the children together and smooth the way for learning.

Building Self-esteem

Classroom bonding also affects self-esteem. "In my older son's kindergarten, one of the favorite activities of all the students was creating birthday books," says Charles James, a father of two. "Every time a child celebrated a birthday in the class, each student was given a sheet of paper and asked to draw a picture of a gift he or she would like to give the birthday person. The teacher then collected the pictures and stapled them together, with a special cover, to create a book. Then the whole class gathered to watch the birthday boy or girl 'open' the presents (by 'reading' the book aloud).

"When his birthday came up, my son was really into Power Rangers, and half the class seemed to know it," says James. "His birthday book was filled with pictures of Power Rangers—especially his favorite: the Red Ranger. He was so touched! I think he got more enjoyment from reading and re-reading that birthday book than he did from his actual presents—because it made him feel like his classmates cared and really were his friends."

This is no minor accomplishment. Most kindergarten teachers say that the better their students feel about classroom friendships, the better they are at learning.

The Call to Independence

Another important element in socialization is building independence. In fact, one of the biggest differences between preschool and kindergarten is in the amount of responsibility the children are given. In kindergarten, they aren't babied as much. They're expected to make more choices, complete more assignments with less out-side help, and follow rules more closely.

According to teachers, many children who are physically capable enter kindergarten expecting adults to do everything. For example, some children will take out their drink and straw and just stare at them, in hopes that the teacher will notice and rush over to help. And more than a few five-year-olds go to school without knowing how to put on their own coats or take care of them-selves in the bathroom.

Part of the problem is that we parents aren't always aware of how much five-year-olds can do. We often feel we still have to feed, clean, and dress our children long after they're capable of doing these things themselves.

I know this from experience. A few weeks after my first son, Gus, went to kindergarten, I woke up one weekend morning to discover that he had made me breakfast. The child I assumed couldn't drink juice from a spill-proof cup without spilling had managed to get a bowl, a glass, and a spoon out of the cupboard, set the table, and pour out cereal, milk, and juice for me—without losing a drop. I was floored. But when I expressed my amazement, he just shrugged his shoulders and said, "We do it all the time at school, Mom."

What Teachers Won't Allow

Even when we *know* what our children are capable of, we often don't require it—because it's easier and faster to do things ourselves. But again, children this age don't really benefit from being babied. And most kindergarten teachers don't allow it.

Their goal is to get their students to do as much as they possibly can for themselves. If a child hands the teacher a bag of chips he can't open, she'll point him to the scissors, for instance. If he can't put on his own jacket, she'll teach him a special little-kid strategy. (You put the jacket on the floor, with the zipper open and facing upward, and the collar or hood near your feet; then you bend over, put your hands into the armholes, and flip the jacket over your head as you stand up.) If he needs help with an assignment while the teacher is busy, she'll tell him to ask a classmate.

This no-nonsense approach isn't always popular at first. But teachers say that once their students begin to see that they *can* do things and solve problems by themselves, they feel great. Their self-esteem soars, and they begin to look at new challenges in a more positive light. Instead of thinking "I'll never be able to do that," they tell themselves: "Here's one more thing I can learn to do myself."

Other Important Subjects

In the midst of all this socialization and independence building, a lot of learning goes on, too. In fact, you may be surprised by just how much academic material is presented—and how it's being taught.

"When I went to kindergarten thirty-odd years ago, there weren't a lot of expectations about what we should or could learn," says Julie Ritzer Ross, a mother of two. "It was just this fun place where you went and played with blocks, did organized crafts, and ate paste. Now that so many children go to preschool, I knew my son Max would probably be doing more in kindergarten than I did. But I was still amazed by how much more he actually did.

"Among other things," says Ross, "my son's kindergarten class learned about French impressionist painters and tried their hands at painting in the style of Monet (though Max was convinced that the artist's name was 'Lo mein'). They also learned how to write and illustrate their own books; count to one hundred fifty by ones, twos, and tens; and weigh, measure, and estimate. Things have really changed since I was a kid," she adds.

General Academic Goals

Different schools have different curriculums, of course. But many kindergarten teachers share similar academic goals. In particular, they want their students to:

- *Develop strong prereading skills.* While a small percentage of children enter kindergarten able to read, or learn to read during the school year, the majority are just beginning to understand the connection between what they say (spoken language) and what they see in books (printed language). So the main focus in kindergarten is on helping kids:

  - recognize all of the letters of the alphabet (in both uppercase and lowercase forms)
  - learn the letter sounds (of both vowels and consonants)
  - identify easy, commonly seen words (including their own names)
  - build their vocabulary
  - feel confident they *can* learn to read
  - develop a deep-rooted love for books.

  Different forms of print—including fiction, nonfiction, poetry, recipes, and songs—are used to develop these skills. And in most classrooms, the environment is saturated with print.

  The ultimate goal, teachers say, is not to make sure that everyone leaves kindergarten being able to read. It's to make sure children gain the knowledge, confidence, and desire to learn—so they can make the big leap in first grade.

- *View themselves as writers.* The first step is teaching children how to form both uppercase and lowercase letters. At this point, however, perfection is not the goal. Many children in this grade reverse their letters (printing *E* backward, for instance), have a hard time printing in a straight line, and make uppercase letters larger than lowercase ones. The point is to learn and practice.

The next step is helping children move from writing letters to writing words, sentences, and stories. But rather than focus on spelling words correctly, most kindergarten teachers concentrate on building a child's belief that he *can* express his feelings, ideas, and opinions in print. So if your child comes home with a story about a "fy dg," focus on his effort ("Wow! You wrote that yourself!"), not the end product ("That's nice, honey, but *funny* has a 'unn' in it, and *dog* is spelled d-o-g"). There will be plenty of time to perfect spelling in first and second grade.

- *Improve their listening and communication skills.* The art of listening is stressed in this grade, mainly because it's crucial to learning in later grades, and most kids don't have a natural knack for it. Listening skills are sharpened through activities that require children to:

    - raise their hand or wait their turn before speaking
    - follow (and sometimes repeat) spoken directions
    - answer questions after someone else has spoken or a book has been read
    - listen to stories, songs, or poems on tape and then tell others about them
    - work with other children to solve a problem or complete a project.

Communication skills—which enhance both learning and social interactions—are developed through activities such as show-and-tell, team projects, and dramatic play. The goal is to help children feel confident about asking questions and expressing their feelings, opinions, and needs to others.

- *Build a concrete awareness of math.* Instead of memorizing math facts (as in 2 + 2 = 4), most kindergartners spend their time on hands-on activities that bring adding, subtracting, and other mathematical functions to life. For example, they might face a problem like this: If you have two Gummy Bears, and your friend gives you two more, how many do you have? To solve it, they might take some actual Gummy Bears out of a package and act out the equation ("I've got two. Now you give me two. Now let's count how many I have").

  Objects (like Gummy Bears) that children can manipulate (known as *manipulatives*) are now used to teach everything from basic math concepts (more than, less than, equal to) to math operations (adding and subtracting) and spatial relationships (top/bottom, above/below, near/far, in front/in back) throughout the elementary years. In kindergarten, children tend to use them for:

  - *sorting and counting* (How many red M&Ms are there? How many blue?)
  - *weighing, measuring, comparing, and graphing* (Whose teddy bear is taller? Which straw is longer? How many kids have juice for lunch, and how many have milk?)
  - *estimating* (How many jelly beans fill this jar?)

- *identifying different patterns and shapes* (If the pattern is red, blue, yellow, what comes after blue? How many squares, circles, rectangles, or other shapes, do you see?)
- *telling time, counting money, keeping track of the calendar, and other real-life number crunching.*

The overall goal is to help children learn to visualize numbers and math concepts (so they can eventually tell, for instance, that there are three jelly beans in your hand, or that one hand has more jelly beans than the other, without having to count out each bean).

- *Acquire an active interest in their world.* Curiosity comes naturally to most kindergartners. But teachers do a lot to build on that curiosity by encouraging their kids to explore, observe, and experiment in a variety of subject areas:

  - *in art and music* the focus is on exposing children to different materials and methods of self-expression
  - *in health and physical education* children learn about how their bodies work and how to keep them healthy and active
  - *in social studies* they're introduced to the major religious and civic holidays and the historical figures behind them (George Washington and Martin Luther King, for example); they're encouraged to explore the similarities and differences among themselves, their fami-

lies, and their traditions; and they learn about their schools, their neighborhoods, and their communities to get a sense of where everything is and what everyone does

- *in science* they're encouraged to recognize and use all of their senses (seeing, hearing, tasting, smelling, and touching) while observing and experimenting with already familiar subjects such as plants and animals, night and day, hot and cold, weather, and space.

Homework—and How to Help

Though homework might have been unheard of when you were in kindergarten, nowadays it's not uncommon. Fortunately, when it's given, it's usually only a couple of times a week. It rarely takes more than fifteen minutes, and it tends to be easy and fun.

Some kindergarten teachers will send home worksheets or ask children to practice printing their numbers and letters. But more often than not these days, homework assignments require children to experiment, explore, observe, or create. For example, your child might be asked to:

- draw a picture that includes three items that begin with the letter *T*

- find three things in the kitchen that begin with the letter *P*

- count the shoes in your house and make a graph to show how many pairs each family member has

- draw a picture of your family mailbox

- have someone read to her for at least fifteen minutes.

Your job is mainly to make the effort to sit with your child as she does her homework. This will not only teach her that you think school is important, it'll keep you informed about what your child is learning and where she needs extra help.

No Need to Push

If your child's teacher doesn't give out homework, or if you think your child is capable of doing more than what the teacher assigns, you may be tempted to ask for extra assignments. Or you may feel like running out and buying workbooks, flash cards, or computer games to keep your child a step ahead. None of that is necessary.

The very best ways to help a five- or six-year-old build reading, writing, and arithmetic skills are to sit with her, talk to her, and play with her. For example, playing board games and card games will help build her math skills, watching you follow a recipe to bake cookies will encourage reading, and telling and writing stories together will build a strong foundation for writing.

Be Sure to Read

The most important homework for kindergarten kids— whether or not it's officially assigned—is: *Read with an adult for at least fifteen minutes every night.* This is something every family should strive for. *Reading is the single most important skill your child must learn to succeed in school.*

You're going to hear that over and over again, not only in this book but from every single teacher your child has from now until fifth grade. Reading is the key that unlocks all learning.

You needn't worry about whether or not your child *can* read at this point. Nor should you be pushing her to learn. There are many different factors that influence when any given child "cracks the code" and becomes a reader. And there are many important steps that lead to that goal (see chapter 7). Your job now is only to expose your child to print and make reading feel like a wonderful experience.

Measuring Progress

Different teachers have different ideas of what they want their students to accomplish by the end of the school year. And many parents have preconceived notions about what their child should achieve ("He should be reading by the end of kindergarten" or "I expect him to be able to add simple numbers"). But the most important gauge of kindergarten success is simply: Has this child shown progress?

"By the end of kindergarten, what your child knows is not nearly as important as how much she's learned and how she feels about herself and school," says Robert McClure, Ph.D., a senior staff member with the National Education Association, based in Washington, D.C. "Young children grow and learn at very different rates," he says. "What one child learns in two years, another might learn in three. So you don't want to compare your child to others. Instead ask, 'Is my child moving forward?' and 'Does she think learning is challenging—and fun?'"

Today's Yardsticks

Since progress is relative, kindergarten teachers now use a variety of tools to measure individual growth. These include developmental checklists, daily journals, written anecdotes, and portfolios of the children's work. To communicate progress, they not only send home report cards, they also schedule face-to-face meetings with parents at regular intervals throughout the year.

In addition, today's report cards tend to be more detailed than what your parents saw when you were a child. Instead of reading statements like "Johnny is a nice boy who behaves well in class" (as they did), you're more likely to see a checklist that addresses specific questions you might have about where your child stands in terms of his:

- *favorite classroom activities* (Does he prefer dramatic play? Art? Writing? Math? Cooking?)

- *typical outdoor pursuits* (Does he prefer interactive games? Climbing? Sand and water play?)

- *status as an independent learner* (Is he taking care of his own needs and seeking help appropriately? Actively exploring classroom materials? Participating in group activities?)

- *development of large and small motor skills* (Is he participating in physical education activities and using all of the playground equipment? Can he use scissors, small building blocks, and drawing utensils?)

- *social interactions and emotional development* (Is he getting along with peers? Following classroom rules? Solving peer conflicts appropriately?)

- *conceptual development* (Where is he in terms of his ability to understand and work with patterns, concepts, and numbers?)

- *language and literacy development* (Which emerging reading and writing skills does he display?).

In addition, there's often at least one page of written comments, and the work saved in your child's portfolio may be reviewed and discussed during parent/teacher conferences.

Preventing Problems

Most teachers don't stop at formal evaluations. If you have *any* concerns about your child's progress at any point in the school year, you should feel free to contact the teacher. Most want to know right away if a child is feeling frustrated or overwhelmed or starts saying that she hates school. Something can usually be done to turn those kinds of feelings around—and the sooner, the better.

Talking to your child's teacher is especially important if you feel your child is not making any progress in a particular academic area, or is having a hard time learning something. Just because the teacher is teaching something in a certain way, it doesn't mean your child should automatically get it. Children learn in different ways, so if one teaching strategy isn't working, another might.

Most teachers have a bag of tricks they can go through

to help children who are having trouble learning something. If that doesn't help, they can consult other specialists in the school (such as the principal, speech therapist, social worker, special education teacher, nurse, psychologist, or math and reading specialists). Often, a team of school professionals will work together in evaluating and planning interventions for a child who needs extra help.

All Problems Welcome

Social and emotional problems should also be brought to a teacher's attention as soon as possible, since they can hinder academic progress if they're not resolved. Plus, solutions tend to come more easily when the parent and the school work together: The child gets a more consistent message about her feelings or behaviors, and the parent gets some much-needed support.

"Halfway through the year, when my first son was in kindergarten, he suddenly refused to get on the bus and go to school," says Mary Mitchell. "It was so unexpected, I didn't know what to do. He put up such a fuss that I decided to let him stay home that day and tried to find out what was bothering him. It didn't help.

"The next day, when he refused to go again, I talked to the bus driver and the teacher to see if they knew why my son might be upset. Neither of them could identify a reason; as far as they could see, Geoff was enjoying school. So the teacher suggested I talk to the school psychologist, who was very helpful. She reassured me that Geoff's behavior was not uncommon and gave me some specific strategies (such as waking him up earlier, so he'd have more time to get ready for school, and giving him some limited choices, so he'd feel more in control of his

life) to minimize the morning battles but still make sure
he got to school. She even encouraged me to send him in
his pajamas if he refused to get dressed on time.

"Her advice, and her moral support, were very important to me," adds Mitchell. "They helped me remain
consistent. It took a couple of weeks, but Geoff did eventually give up the fight about going to school. Ever since
then, I've felt very comfortable talking to my kids' teachers whenever I have any questions or concerns about
school. I don't always agree with what they say, but I do
try to keep the lines of communication open."

What to Expect on the Social Scene

Lots of play dates. Though most kindergarten kids still
relish the warmth and security of home, they're also now
ready to really reach out and play with peers. "Though
my son Max had been having play dates since he was
three," says Julie Ritzer Ross, "it wasn't until kindergarten that he really began wanting to be with his
friends more and wanting to have a best friend."

Many children start the school year by playing with
kids they already know from their preschool, bus, or
neighborhood. If encouraged to branch out and form new
alliances, however, many happily will. Kindergarten kids
tend to be very accepting. They're willing to play with
lots of different children, and they aren't as biased
against girl/boy play as eight- and nine-year-olds can be.

Branching Out

The key is encouragement, however. That's why most
kindergarten teachers spend a great deal of time helping

children navigate social terrain. They work on getting shy children to feel brave enough to join in during group activities; teaching awkward children how to behave and what to say, so their classmates will want to play with them; and helping "best friends" expand their social contacts.

"When my son, James, went to kindergarten, it seemed like the first two weeks were focused on friendship issues," says Ronald Kern, a father of two. "The teacher read books to the class about making friends and spent a lot of time reinforcing the idea that all of the children in the class were friends. My son, who had been nervous about not having a friend when school started, just lapped it all up. By the third week, when I asked him who his friends were at school, he said, 'Everyone, of course!'"

In many classrooms, there's even a special day—usually the 100th day of school—to celebrate being friends. Together, the children keep track of the school days (by adding a macaroni noodle to a jar each day, for instance). Then, when the 100th day comes, they have a party and do all sorts of 100-related things. For instance, they might make necklaces from 100 Froot Loops, decorate a cake with 100 M&Ms, or create collections of 100 objects.

What Friendship Means

It's important to remember, however, that a kindergartner's version of friendship is often radically different from an adult's. At this age, friendships are very fluid. Children are just coming out of the parallel play period (when they tend to play alongside, but not exactly with, another child). And they're just beginning to learn how to get along with peers in both one-on-one and group situations.

Not all children find "best friends" in kindergarten. And in many cases, when they do, the "two's company, three's a crowd" mentality exists. So if you throw three kids together on a play date, two of them will team up and refuse to play with the third or, even worse, will taunt him (with timeless childhood stingers like "You're just a crybaby!" and "You're not our friend").

However, the "best friend" of today may become the fifth wheel tomorrow—for no apparent reason. So if you hear things like "Ashley doesn't like me anymore" or "Billy always hits me," don't panic. And don't get too concerned if your child fights a lot with his friends. As Julie Ritzer Ross notes, "My son's current best friend is a little boy he met on the first day of kindergarten and took a shine to. The two of them love to play together after school, but they also tend to fight a lot over little things— like who gets to use the computer next. It used to worry me when they fought, but then I noticed that their conflicts usually last for less than five minutes, and neither of them ever carries a grudge when a fight is over. They forget about it and move on to the next activity."

Resolving Conflicts

When conflicts occur, try not to take them too seriously. Otherwise, you might end up getting too involved in your child's squabbles, and he might turn into a tattletale. Or you might end up making a bad situation worse. Parents will often start battling with each other because their kids aren't getting along. But then the kids will get over it—and the parents won't.

A better way to help is to stand back and play a supportive role. If your child is upset about something a classmate did or said, for instance, don't keep pumping for details or start threatening to tell the teacher. Instead, ask your child questions he can learn from, such as:

- How did you handle that?
- How did it make you feel?
- Is there something you might have done to make that person mad?
- What do you think you could do the next time it happens?

Those are the kinds of questions teachers ask in their classrooms daily to build conflict-resolution skills. The goal is not just to keep the classroom peaceful. It's to help children figure out ways to say what they feel and want, rather than crying or hitting.

Teachers also work on giving children the exact words they need to use. For example, instead of suggesting that two kids "talk it out" when one kid hits the other because she called him a dummy, they'll say: "We do not hit our friends. The next time she calls you a dummy, tell her right away that she's hurting your feelings and you want her to stop."

Copycat Kids

Another peer-related trend you'll probably notice in kindergarten is the desire to mimic friends. "Kindergarten is when my son, Jack, first began to think about who the 'cool' kids in the class were, and began to want to be like them," says Tamara Eberlein. "For instance, when one child he particularly admired got *Star Wars* sneakers, Jack came home and announced that he needed them, too."

Good kindergarten teachers understand this and are able to channel this impulse to enhance learning. They'll put four or five children together at a table and give them a project, for instance, and then sit back and watch the ideas fly.

One child might say, "I know how to spell *love.* I'm going to write the word *love* on my picture," for example. Then, the next thing you know, everyone at the table wants to write the word *love,* and another child is saying, "Look! I can draw a heart right next to the word *love!*"

Picking Up Bad Habits

Don't expect everything your child learns from peers to be pleasant, however. As Mary Mitchell notes, "Sometimes Max will pick up words or rhymes from his classmates and busmates that aren't entirely appropriate—words we'd never use at home. But I've learned to accept that that's what happens when you send kids to school. And I just tell him, 'We don't use words like that in our house.'"

Another very common—and very annoying—habit kids often pick up in kindergarten is talking like a baby. In fact, baby talk can spread through a classroom like wildfire. It starts with one child and before you know it they're all doing it. So when it first appears, it's a good idea to be strict about saying "I need you to use your five-year-old voice."

The After-School Schedule

When planning your kindergartner's after-school activities, it's important to keep things simple. According to teachers, too many parents fall into the trap of thinking that early achievement is everything—and end up over-booking their child. One or two extracurricular activities a week is plenty; for daily after-school care, the less structure there is, the better.

Even in half-day kindergartens, most children get plenty of math and reading during the school day. After-school time should be spent on creative and physical pursuits, such as art projects, music or dance lessons, and athletics. But even running around a playground with friends is enough.

Let Your Child Relax

A key consideration is your child's energy level. By the end of the school day, especially with full-day programs, most kindergarten kids are tuckered out. And not just physically. It takes a lot of emotional energy to behave, learn, and interact with the other children all day. That's why kindergarten kids often get home from school and act irritable or have meltdowns.

The toughest time is the beginning of the school year, when all the new adjustments are being made. So you may want to hold off on after-school lessons and classes until October or November, when your child is more used to the school routine and has more energy to spare.

*I*f kindergarten is the year when children learn how to go to school, first grade is when serious learning begins.

"It's not that children don't learn in kindergarten," explains Katy Musolino, a mother of two. "It's just that in first grade, the academic expectations become greater. There's a lot more work mixed in with the fun."

Fortunately, by first grade most children are physically, emotionally, and intellectually ready to handle more-serious schoolwork. But that doesn't mean you should expect the transition to be trouble-free.

A TIME OF GREAT CHANGE

For most kids, going to first grade means adjusting to a variety of changes. It may involve moving to a new, larger school; taking the bus for the first time; or expanding from a half-day program to a full-day one. It may also mean spending more time sitting at a desk doing paper-work; moving around the school for special classes (in art, music, and gym); and mixing with older, more intim-idating children (at recess and lunchtime). At the very least, there'll be a new teacher and some unfamiliar faces on the first day of school.

These kinds of changes can be overwhelming to a six-or seven-year-old, so it's important to be patient and sup-portive when this more serious school year begins. Your child may be more emotional than usual, more anxious about academic performance, or more exhausted at the end of the school day. You may even see some regression in behavior (a renewal of thumb sucking, for instance, or a reacquaintance with temper tantrums). But the good news is, it won't last long.

Once your child gets the hang of first grade, you'll see a big jump in maturity and self-esteem. As Terri Palma, a mother of two, notes, "At the beginning of first grade, my daughter Chloe was a little overwhelmed by the full-day schedule. She really enjoyed school, but she'd come home feeling tired. By October, she had a lot more energy."

What First Graders Are Like

In many ways, first graders are merely more grown-up versions of kindergarten kids. They're somewhat larger and more competent, of course, but their leading quali-ties are similar. The difference is that six- and seven-year-olds take every behavior to a new height.

For example, they're:

- *Eager to learn.* Teachers say first graders are like lit-tle sponges. "They get so incredibly excited when they master a new skill," explains Rae Ann Gremel, a teacher at Philip R. Smith School in South Windsor, Connecticut. "And they're interested in absolutely everything. All you have to do is pull down a map or start talking about a science project, and they act like you gave them a pot of gold."

They're also curious, energetic, full of surprises, and thrilled to be in school, say other teachers. And by now they're really primed for learning. Whereas kindergarten kids are mainly involved in absorbing how to do things and put things together, first graders are beginning to make connections. They're starting to see how bits of information from previous experiences can be used to solve problems and develop ideas of their own. For example, if the teacher reads the class a book about pirates and treasure maps, a few days later a child might decide to draw his friend a map to help him find a toy that's been hidden in the classroom.

- *Eager to try.* First graders are still at an age when they believe they can do *anything*. And they're not, for the most part, embarrassed to take risks. So you still see a lot of creativity and self-expression in the classroom.

  You also see a lot of pride. Whereas younger children get much of their pleasure from simply *doing* something (like painting a picture or playing with blocks), first graders have just as much fun showing off what they've done.

- *Eager to please.* Even though they're more independent and outspoken than kindergartners, first graders are still committed to pleasing their parents and teacher. They love being told exactly what's expected of them. And once they comply, they like to hear that you've noticed and approve.

Teachers capitalize on this by using lots of positive reinforcement in the classroom. If a child is standing quietly in line or following directions, for instance, the teacher might comment aloud, "Look how nicely Janis is standing in line" or "I appreciate the way Janis is doing exactly what I asked." As soon as the other children hear that, they start thinking, "I can do that, too. In fact, I think I will—so the teacher will notice me and think I'm wonderful, too."

Be forewarned, however, that the desire to please may be stronger at school than at home. Most first graders adore their teacher and regard her or him as the ultimate authority. In fact, you'll probably get tired of hearing "My teacher said this" and "My teacher told us that" this year. But, at this age, it's good for children to respect their teacher and think of her word as law. It helps them adjust more quickly to the demands and routines of school.

The More-Trying Traits

Like kindergartners, first graders love to talk (especially about themselves), and they love to win. In fact, most of them want to be the first in everything—whether it's standing in line or getting the most answers correct on a test. It's not that they're selfish. It's just that it doesn't occur to them that the other twenty-two or so kids in the class might want or deserve the exact same thing.

That's especially true when it comes to getting the

teacher's attention. "If I'm working with one child, another one will walk right up to us, stand in front of me, and just start talking," notes Kim Reichert of the Kew-Forest School in Forest Hills, New York. "They all want the teacher all to themselves, so you really have to work on getting them to be polite and wait their turn."

The Blame Game

You also have to work on discouraging tattling and blaming, which tend to blossom in first grade. As children become more aware of the rules of proper behavior, they also become more vigilant about who's breaking which rule. And if they're not the person at fault, their immediate demand is for justice.

Of course, when *they* stand accused, there's always a reason *why* the misbehavior happened ("He pushed me out of line!"or "She's talking too loud and I can't think!"). Teachers even hear excuses like "My mom wouldn't let me do my homework"—not because first graders enjoy lying, but because they're still at an age when fantasy and reality sometimes mix.

Intense Emotions

Conflicts also occur because most first graders have fragile emotions. If someone laughs at them, calls them stupid, or says they don't want to be their friend, for instance, they feel crushed. They're too inexperienced to know that those kinds of things happen to everyone.

And they aren't very good at hiding their feelings. They'll cry when they're hurt, for instance; they'll yell, hit, or throw a tantrum when they're frustrated or angry;

and they'll bite their nails, chew on their clothes, crack their knuckles, grind their teeth, or even wet their pants if they're anxious. First graders have a lot going on in their lives, and they can't always cope gracefully with the stress.

Consistency Helps

So don't be surprised if one minute your child is acting with unexpected maturity, and the next minute is reacting with unexpected tears. It's totally normal for this grade. And it may help to know that most kids this age behave better at school than at home. If something upsets them, they'll hold themselves together in front of the teacher—and then fall apart as soon as they're safely at home.

It helps to be consistent, especially with daily routines. First graders feel most comfortable when they know exactly what's going to happen next. That's why most teachers spend a lot of time in the beginning of the school year just talking about why the children are in school and how they need to behave in order for everyone to be able to learn.

What First Graders Should Know

There are no set standards for first grade entrance. What teachers say they most like to see in all of the students who enter their classrooms is strong self-esteem and a positive attitude toward learning. The better a child feels about himself and school, they say, the more likely he is to keep moving ahead.

It'll also help if your child is:

- *Ready to read.* That doesn't mean she should actually be reading. But she should be able to recognize (and make the sounds of) various letters of the alphabet. She should understand that letters can be combined to make words, and that written words are a printed form of language. She should be familiar enough with books to understand the left-to-right progression in reading, and be able to "read" a story by looking at its pictures.

  Many children, by now, can also read (and write) their first name, as well as some short, frequently seen words (such as *the, to,* and *go*). But even more important is being aware of and curious about all sorts of print—from books, magazines, and newspapers to traffic signs, menus, store signs, cereal boxes, and even toy packaging.

- *Aware of numbers.* This includes being able to count (at least up to twenty); recognize written numbers (at least up to ten); and tell when one number is bigger or smaller than another. Some kids can do some very simple addition and subtraction, but it's not expected. What teachers look for is an understanding of one-to-one correspondence (that the numeral 3 means three objects, for instance) and the ability to create a model of a simple equation. For example, if the teacher says "Sherrie has three Barbies. If she gives one to her younger sister, how many will she have left?" your child should know that she could find the answer by putting out three objects (or raising three fingers) and taking one away.

  Being aware of how numbers are used in our daily lives (on clocks, calendars, addresses, price tags, and

speed limit signs, for example) is also important. And
teachers like to see first graders who know their own
age, birth date, phone number, and address.

- *Able to focus.* It's no longer enough for a child to just
  sit in a group and behave. He has to be able to focus
  on whatever's being taught, so he can learn, participate in the discussion, and follow directions.

  Many children enter first grade with only a five-to-
  ten-minute attention span—and that's fine for a starting point. But the better your child gets at filtering
  out distractions, paying attention, and following
  directions, the easier first grade will seem.

Expect Diversity

In all of these areas, some children are further ahead by
first grade, while others are a bit behind. And even individual children may be advanced for their grade in one
area (say, reading) and behind their peers in another
(such as math). In most cases, however, there's no need to
worry. Though academic expectations are higher in first
grade, teachers still see a broad spectrum of abilities and
behavior. And, as in kindergarten, their focus is on
progress, not performance.

If you have any concerns about your child's readiness,
contact both her kindergarten teacher and the first grade
teacher in her school. In most cases, the teachers will be
more concerned about separation and social skills than
academic ability. But if there are learning gaps, they
should be addressed.

Nowadays, many educators prefer not to retain (hold
back) children, because some research shows it can have a

negative effect on self-esteem. Instead, if a child is lagging in a particular subject area, the first step is often arranging for enrichment activities at home and/or special tutoring at school. If that doesn't help, the teacher may recommend that your child undergo some form of testing to determine how best to meet his or her educational needs.

What to Expect in the Classroom

Depending on where your child goes to school, first grade may or may not look a lot like kindergarten. In many schools, the hands-on, open-ended, and integrated approaches offered in kindergarten are merely taken to more challenging levels in first grade. The classroom may still have no formal desks, for example. Instead, you might see a large, carpeted area where the students gather periodically throughout the day—for group lessons, strategy meetings, show-and-tell activities, and other important events—and long tables for seat work.

Many first grade classrooms also have a:

- special library area, with comfortable seating (a couch, pillows, or bean bags) and lots of books and books-on-tape geared to various reading levels

- a "writing center" stocked with paper, pencils, pens, markers, crayons, alphabet stamps, scissors, glue, staplers, and other materials for producing stories and books

- a "math center" with games, flash cards, and manipulatives (tangible objects—such as teddy bear counters, plastic links, pattern blocks, dice, buttons, and pennies—that children can use to sort, classify, measure, estimate, weigh, and model simple addition and subtraction problems)

- a "science center" featuring books, equipment for classroom experiments, plants, and sometimes even living creatures. (In my older son's first grade classroom, the children worked alongside a tarantula, a ball python, an iguana, a mouse, turtles, fish, a chameleon, and a cockatiel, which spent most of its day perched on the teacher's shoulder.)

- a computer corner, with one or two terminals offering simple educational games that reinforce basic math and reading skills.

As in kindergarten, the classroom walls are usually plastered with colorful posters. There's some sort of banner in the front of the room with all the letters of the alphabet, in uppercase and lowercase forms; some sort of numbers chart; and various samples of the children's work.

More Traditional Settings

Not all schools follow this model, however. In fact, in many cases, first grade is when the classroom takes a more traditional turn. The students sit at assigned desks for the first time (though they're often arranged in clusters of four or more, instead of rows). And they may spend more time in their seats, using soft-cover standardized reading and math workbooks, instead of moving around the classroom and doing hands-on projects in learning centers.

In most cases, however, it's not so much the classroom layout as the classroom leader that really counts. As one father notes, "My son, who's in fifth grade now, has been in both traditional and nontraditional classrooms. And in each case, it was the quality of the teacher, and the chemistry between the teacher and my son, that determined whether or not he had a successful school year."

Different Ways to Learn

Your child's individual learning style can also make a difference. Some children are more adept at learning when they can get information visually—by watching a demonstration, for instance, or looking at a picture, a video, or a three-dimensional object. Others learn more efficiently through auditory or hands-on experiences. Some do better with sequence and structure, while others take a more circuitous route toward understanding.

Different classrooms (and schools) often favor different learning styles. And some parents have seen their children get "turned around" by moving from one environment to another. Even within the same family, one child might do better in a more unstructured, open-ended classroom, while another might thrive in a more traditional setting.

Some schools offer more than one type of classroom to suit different learning styles. At one school my son attended in Ohio, for instance, the range included:

- *A fairly traditional first grade classroom,* where students sat in rows of desks and the teacher did most of her teaching from the front of the classroom. These children were in a "looping" program, which means they stayed with the same group of students and the same teacher for both first and second grade. Then the students moved on to third grade and the teacher went back to leading a first grade class.

- *Two multi-age, nongraded classrooms,* each of which included both first and second grade students, who were given work based not on their traditional grade levels, but on their individual abilities. (In other words, a first grade–level student who was ahead in math might be given the second grade–level math worksheets.) Instead of sitting at assigned desks, the children would sit in a circle on the floor for class meetings and group lessons, and do their reading, math, and other pencil-and-paper work at tables or clustered desks. Those who entered the classroom as first graders would stay in the same room, with the same teacher, for the second grade year. Second-year students who had completed the second grade–level curriculum were promoted to third grade.

- *A nongraded, open classroom* that combined two classes' worth of first and second graders in one wide-open space (two traditional classrooms with the wall between them torn down) and featured two teachers (team teaching). In this room, there were no desks, lots of learning centers, and an integrated curriculum with a fine arts theme. Students who entered as first graders typically spent two years in this class before moving on to third grade.

If your child's school offers more than one type of learning environment, it's worth it to make an appointment to observe them all and measure each one against your child's individual learning style. If you don't have a choice, however, don't get discouraged. Though diverse in appearance and approach, most first grade classrooms are designed to meet similar academic goals. And, again, it's often the teacher, not the classroom layout, that makes the most difference.

A Quiet Hum

One more thing: If you visit a first grade classroom when the students are in it, you'll probably notice it's noisier than what you remember from first grade. The reason is that educators now believe children can learn a lot from each other. So in all of the subject areas, teachers today build in lots of opportunities for cooperative work.

Working with partners or in groups helps children in many different ways, teachers say. It not only enables them to motivate and learn from each other, it gives them invaluable practice in communicating their ideas, listening to others, negotiating, compromising, and getting along. So, as one teacher notes, "You should expect to hear a quiet hum."

The Most Important Subject This Year

Ask most parents and you'll find that their biggest concern at the beginning of first grade is reading. "I was very anxious about when my son John would begin to read," says Katy Musolino. "His older sister had learned to read in kindergarten and was much further along when she entered first grade. So I had lots of questions: Was John slow for his age? Would he be behind his classmates? Would he need a tutor? I wasn't sure what to expect when first grade began, but I knew that reading would be a major focus for all of us."

Ask any teacher and you're likely to sense a similar degree of passion about reading. "As a first grade teacher, I feel I have to do everything short of standing on my head to make sure that every child in the class gets a good start in reading," says Marcia Kenyon of Eastwood Elementary School in West Fargo, North Dakota. "If a child sneaks through first grade without learning to read, it can handicap him for the rest of his years in school."

The Wide Range of Normal

That's not to say that every single child is expected to leave first grade reading at a particular level. As in kindergarten, the range of normal development is incredibly wide in first grade. Teachers say they see everything from the six-year-old who can read at a fifth grade level to the child who doesn't know her alphabet and hasn't quite figured out how to hold a book.

But the *majority* of children enter first grade being *ready* to read. And during the school year, most learn to decode the words they see in print and move on to reading simple books. A small percentage really take off and are able to master more difficult chapter books. And a third group of children simply strengthen their prereading skills, so they can jump on the bandwagon in second grade.

Where your child falls along the reading continuum is less important than whether or not she makes progress in reading in first grade. If she enters as a nonreader and exits as a reader, that's great. If she's a timid reader but becomes a fluent reader, that's great, too.

Learning to read is a very individual, developmental process. And early reading doesn't necessarily translate to better comprehension—or greater school success.

How Reading Is Taught

Teachers today use a variety of tools and strategies to develop reading skills. Among the most prominent are:

- *Phonics.* This is basically the same "sounding out" method of teaching reading that you probably grew up with. (Remember the worksheets that had you "Circle any pictures on this page that begin with the letter *T*"?) The emphasis in phonics is on teaching children about letters, letter sounds, syllables, and words before involving them in reading, writing, or spelling.

  Phonics has come under attack in recent years, for being "too limiting" and "too boring" for most children. Some educators complain that since it teaches words out of context, it helps with decoding but not comprehension. Others, however, insist that it's still the best method for building a strong foundation for reading, writing, and spelling.

  Chances are, phonics won't be the main focus in your child's classroom, but it will play some role in the reading curriculum.

- *Basal readers.* These textbooks (and workbooks) use stories with controlled vocabularies to guide children, in a step-by-step manner, from simple to complex reading skills. They stress the development of a "sight word" vocabulary, in which children memorize whole words through repetition and practice. You may remember the

"Dick and Jane" readers from your own school days. Today's versions work on the same principles but are somewhat more with it: The stories are more interesting, more ethnically diverse, and more literary.

You're most likely to find basal readers in fairly traditional school settings and in classrooms where the phonics approach is used. However, many "whole language" (see below) teachers keep a set of them available for students who learn best from a sequential approach. And some teachers say they use them just to make doubly sure they cover all of the important reading-related bases. As one teacher notes, "I don't rely on the basal readers, but I do use them because they help me keep track of all the specific skills the children have been exposed to."

- *Whole language.* This is the newest approach to teaching reading. Instead of focusing on letter sounds, syllables, and words first, teachers who favor whole language immerse their students in books, stories, and poems written by well-known authors of children's literature. In addition, the traditional approach of dividing children up into skill-related reading groups and teaching reading for one period a day is replaced by an effort to integrate reading, writing, telling, and listening skills into every single subject area.

  During a science unit on mammals, for instance, a child might read nonfiction books about her favorite mammal, prepare a brief report about where it lives and what it likes to eat, and deliver that report to her classmates.

  In whole language settings, children are also encouraged to write their own books, and printed words appear all over the classroom. The idea is that young children learn to read by being read to, by reading literature that's related to real life, and by reading and writing as much as possible. When they encounter an unfamiliar word, they're taught to figure it out by looking for clues in the text and the pictures, rather than just sounding out the letters.

Interesting subject matter is an essential component in the whole language approach. Instead of expecting every child in the class to be engaged by the stories in a standardized reading text, whole language teachers encourage children to choose books that appeal to their individual skills and interests. The goal is to make reading seem relevant and pleasurable, even to the most reluctant readers.

Not everyone in education believes in whole language. Its critics claim that it doesn't build a strong enough foundation in spelling and grammar and provides insufficient tools for decoding unfamiliar and difficult words. But most first grade teachers have taken at least some steps to fill their classroom bookshelves with really great children's literature and to integrate more reading and writing into other subject areas.

The Best Approach

You may find that your child's teacher is devoted to one of these tools or strategies. But in most classrooms today, you're likely to see various elements of each. The reason is simple: Experienced classroom teachers know that no two children learn how to read in exactly the same way.

That's why you'll also see a variety of reading-related activities, such as:

- *Chunking.* The teacher holds up a flash card with a common letter cluster, such as *at* on it. Then she adds another with a consonant (such as *h*) to form a word (*hat*). She then removes the consonant card and adds another, to form a different word (such as *bat*, *sat*, or *cat*). Each time the children read the new word aloud, they begin to see how words in the same "family" tend to look alike and rhyme.

- *Patterning.* While reading a big (oversized) book to the class, the teacher asks the children to look for patterns in both the words (that is, words that are repeated regularly or rhyme) and the sentences (for instance, each new page of the book might begin with the same phrase: "My favorite fruit is yellow"; "My favorite shirt is blue"; and so on). Children are later asked to use the dominant sentence pattern ("My favorite _____ is _____ ") to write their own books.

- *Sequencing.* Children are given a series of pictures and are asked to put them in the right order, to tell a coherent story (first you bake the cake, then you put on the candles and sing "Happy Birthday," then you eat the cake, then you clean up). As reading skills develop, children might be asked to arrange a series of sentence strips into a proper sequence.

- *Memorizing.* The teacher keeps on a bulletin board a list of simple, common "sight" words (such as *his*, *her*, *stop*, *of*, and *again*) that the students need to memorize, so they can recognize them on sight in a text. For homework, children are given flash cards to help them memorize words that'll appear in the next day's readings. This helps build a sight word vocabulary and leads to confidence when encountering a new text.

- *Partner reading.* Two children are assigned to read a book together and help each other out with unfamiliar words. Or, a more advanced reader in the class is asked to read with a beginner-level one.

- *Literary chats.* A small group of children gather to discuss the plot, characters, setting, and so forth of a book they've all read.

- *D.E.A.R. time.* Children are instructed to "*D*rop *E*verything *A*nd *R*ead" on their own, silently, for fifteen or so minutes at some point during every school day. This period might be known by other names, such as G.R.A.B. time (as in "*G*o *R*ead *A* *B*ook") or S.S.R. time (for "*S*ustained *S*ilent *R*eading").

Helping a Slow Starter

If you notice that your child is not making progress in reading or seems way behind his classmates, don't panic. Remind yourself that different children learn to read in different ways and at different rates. Plus, reading problems can stem from many sources, including vision, memory, and processing problems; lack of exposure to print; poor motivation; and anxiety about failing.

But do bring it up with the teacher. Find out what her approach and expectations are. If they don't fit your child—or if your child doesn't fit them—ask for extra help. Many schools will arrange for a reading specialist or some type of tutoring to get a child over a hump. Or, the teacher may be willing to try new teaching strategies within the classroom setting.

"When I first found out what the first grade teachers in my daughter's school expected in terms of reading, I was concerned," says Terri Palma. "I thought, 'How will we accomplish all of that this year? Chloe's just beginning to learn to read!' But after talking to Chloe's teacher, I felt reassured. She arranged for Chloe to spend twenty minutes a day with a reading tutor, and it made a huge difference. By November, my daughter was reading beginner books, and by February, more complex ones. Her progress has been amazing."

Don't Be Bashful

If talking to the teacher doesn't help, write a letter to the school principal and request that your child be formally tested. There may be a learning disability or a language, development, vision, or hearing problem that's affecting your child's ability to learn how to read. And the sooner it's discovered, the better.

Not all teachers have the experience and/or the training to recognize learning disabilities and developmental problems. In addition, in large classes, teachers don't always pick up on the special needs of every individual child. So if you have concerns, you shouldn't be shy about asking for testing.

At the very least, a formal evaluation may be able to

reassure you that your child is right where he should be, based on his individual pattern of development.

Writing

As important as it is, reading is only one element in a strong first grade "language arts" program. The other major focus in this grade—and this may surprise you—is writing.

You probably remember learning *how* to write (or print) in first grade. That still happens. But nowadays, children also learn how to put their thoughts and ideas onto paper—sometimes even *before* they learn to read.

Among other things, your first grader may be:

- keeping a daily journal, a book journal, or even a math or science journal
- writing stories, poems, and books—alone or with her classmates
- writing brief book reports
- writing sentences to go along with weekly spelling words
- meeting with other "authors" in the classroom to share and critique written work.

In addition, many teachers today integrate as much writing as possible into the overall curriculum.

Impressive Results

Most parents aren't prepared for this new emphasis on early writing. "I was amazed by how much more writing they do in first grade, compared to when I was a kid," says Holly Hughes, a mother of three. "I remember practicing printing; my six-year-old is already keeping a journal!"

Even teachers are sometimes amazed. "When I started teaching first grade, some twenty-five years ago, it was thought that children weren't ready to do any kind of writing until about the second half of the school year," says Rae Ann Gremel. "Now we start them on the very first day—and it's incredible what they can produce: stories, poems, even books that have a distinct beginning, middle, and end."

Starting earlier makes a lot of sense, she adds, since writing reinforces reading skills, and vice versa.

What to Expect

By now you're probably wondering how in the world teachers can get kids who can barely read to write their own books. It's simple: They don't worry about spelling. They encourage their students to jot down whatever parts of a word they can, or "invent" spellings for the words they don't know.

For example, many teachers will start their students writing on the first day of school by handing out journals and saying: "Write about something you like." In a typical first grade classroom, some children will write down five or six letters that represent different parts of the words they want to write ("I l cts" for "I like cats" for instance). Others will connect three or four partial words together ("Ilkcts"), and some will just stare at the page, wanting to cry.

But most teachers will stress that *anything* a child writes down—even if it's only the first letter of each word—is okay. Later, the teacher might ask each student to dictate his or her journal entry, so she can rewrite it the correct way.

As the year progresses and the children gain more experience working with letters, letter sounds, words, and different forms of print, their writing and spelling naturally improve. They begin using more letters in each word (writing "lik" instead of "l" for instance) and writing longer, more complete sentences.

Where Spelling Fits In

Don't worry. Spelling is not totally neglected in first grade. Mistakes do get corrected. And many students still take home lists of words to memorize for weekly spelling tests. In some classrooms, the words are part of a prepackaged reading program; in others, the teacher or the children themselves decide on which spelling words they need to work on. But with creative writing assignments, spelling is not the initial focus.

Instead, teachers want children to see the connection between thinking something and writing it down. And they want them to feel confident that they *can* write. "Worries about spelling often slow kids down," says Jill Mermelstein, of Glenallan Elementary School, in Silver Spring, Maryland. "And it can restrict creativity. I once had a girl who wrote a story about a 'bad dog,' because those were words she knew how to spell. But when she was talking about her story, she described the dog as 'ferocious.'" Most teachers would rather see a child misspell a complex word than rely on a simple one just because he can spell it.

Give It Time

If you're not convinced the first time your child brings home a paper that says "I lv sk" instead of "I love school," don't panic. Talk to the teacher about his or her overall writing curriculum and goals. And give the process time to unfold.

"When my son first started bringing home stories with all the words misspelled, the copy editor in me protested," says Holly Hughes. "I'd see comments from the teacher like, 'You did a great job giving details' or 'Your story really made me laugh,' but nothing like, 'This is the correct way to spell *dinosaur.*' I was very concerned. But as time went on, I noticed my son's spelling was improving—along with his writing. Now I'm just so impressed by how much confidence Hugh has as a writer. He feels completely comfortable putting his thoughts onto paper."

"My daughter is so proud of her writing," says Terri Palma. "They have a 'publishing house' in her school, where the children can go twice a year to have a story they've written typed and bound into a book. They even put an 'About the Author' page at the end. When my daughter got her first book—*Chloe's Cats* by Chloe Palma—published, she was so excited she carried it around for a day and a half; then she immediately started working on her next book. I never did *anything* like that in first grade!"

A Word About Penmanship

As your child's ability to express herself on paper improves, so should her penmanship. Learning how to form letters and stay within the lines is still an important focus in first grade. Different schools use different penmanship programs to teach children how to print, so you should support whichever strategy your child's teacher uses.

But be aware that the ability to print is linked not only to instruction, but to development. Look for practice, not perfection.

The Other Language Arts

As in kindergarten, teachers still spend a great deal of time helping children sharpen their listening and speaking skills, because both contribute to literacy. Activities often include:

- regular class meetings where children brainstorm ideas, plan out projects, or compare notes

- small-group assignments that require team members to work together toward a common goal

- show-and-tell activities that give each child a chance to stand in the spotlight, talk about an interest, and answer classmates' questions

- listening games, in which children must follow verbal directions, or repeat the patterns (in clapping or other body movements) that they see or hear.

Other Important Subjects

Though reading and writing tend to take center stage

in first grade, the other academic subjects are not ignored. In fact, in nearly every school, teachers have an outline of basic information that must be covered in every single subject area, from science to gym. But this "core curriculum" varies from school to school. To get specifics, you'll need to speak to your child's teacher or principal.

In the meantime, here's a general look at what to expect.

Math

Your child *will* be doing math. But you may be surprised at how much more fun—and sophisticated—his math lessons are compared to when you were a kid. Instead of poring over a worksheet with addition and subtraction problems, he may be exchanging pennies for nickels and dimes; creating patterns with blocks in different colors and shapes; or measuring the distance from one side of the classroom to the other in jump ropes, rods, or cubes.

It may look like play. But this hands-on approach is very purposeful. And it's surprisingly broad. Along with teaching adding and subtracting, it gets first graders involved in:

- describing and comparing shapes
- collecting and graphing data
- recognizing numbers up to 100
- working with place values
- counting money and making change
- telling time
- working with fractions
- measuring and estimating.

The New Focus

By switching the focus from memorizing math facts to working with math manipulatives, teachers hope to help their students develop a deeper understanding of mathematical concepts. It used to be that children were taught what the math rules were, and then told to follow them while doing endless worksheets. Now they learn the *why* behind the rules, so that math will seem more meaningful and relevant to their daily lives.

In addition, teachers stress the importance of creative thinking. It's no longer enough for first graders to find the right answer to a math problem: They also have to be able to explain how and why they got it.

Traditional-minded parents needn't worry, however: Worksheets are still used to build computation skills in many classrooms. And most teachers still encourage a certain degree of memorization. Each week, in my son's first grade class, for instance, the children were given "Pocket Facts"—little slips of paper with simple math facts ($8 + 5 = 13$ for example) to carry around in their pockets and memorize.

Science

As in math, the focus in science is on hands-on activities that help children develop their thinking and problem-solving skills. In some classrooms, there is a "science center" where children can engage in a variety of experiments; in others, the class works together on various science projects, such as growing beans, caring for classroom animals, hatching butterflies or chicks, cooking, or keeping track of the weather. And in most classrooms, field trips and scientific visitors round out the program.

The themes tend to be things children can easily identify with, such as animals, plants, and the human body. The overall goal is not so much to fill kids' heads with facts, but to teach them how to think like little scientists. When they perform an experiment, for example, they're encouraged to ask questions; predict what will happen; record or keep track of what they observe; and evaluate their results.

Reading and writing will probably play important roles in your child's science studies. Among other things, she may be asked to keep a science journal, make graphs for various science projects, or take home some nonfiction children's books to "research" a topic of special interest.

Social Studies

Social studies themes vary from school to school. In general, the focus remains on subjects close to home: the family, the neighborhood, the community, the town. However, in some schools, teachers also branch out to how children live in other cultures or how they lived in past times. Some geography is taught, and children often begin learning how to work with simple maps.

Again, the focus is not on filling kids' heads with facts. It's on exposing them to different ways of thinking and living, and encouraging them to ask questions and find answers.

Fine Arts

In many schools, first grade is when children first begin leaving their "base" classroom to spend time in the art room with a specially trained art teacher and in the music room with a teacher skilled in music education. In other schools, the specialists in art and music visit the first graders in their own classroom, while the regular teacher takes a break.

There is, of course, no standard curriculum for what children learn in either art or music. But in most first grades, the focus is on exposing children to both of these subject areas in some way and encouraging them to experiment and express themselves with different artistic materials and instruments.

In art, for example, children might learn about the different kinds of visual effects created by using various patterns, shapes, colors, textures, and art materials; in music they may learn about pitch, rhythm, and volume by listening to and singing different types of songs and trying out various instruments. Dramatic expression and creative movement may also be introduced.

Within the Classroom

Most first grade teachers also try to give their students lots of opportunities for creative expression in the classroom. The children might use their art skills in illustrating a book they've written, or in designing a diorama for a social studies unit, for instance; they might use their music skills when learning a counting song or listening to stories and poems that are set to music.

Physical Education

Depending on where your child goes to school, he may have gym every single day, or only once or twice a week. In general, the more often, the better. Children this age are in constant motion, so they need regular times when they can get out of the classroom and move around.

The emphasis in physical education will probably be threefold:

1. Improving body control (in terms of balance, flexibility, and speed, for instance)
2. Sharpening gross motor skills (running, jumping, climbing, etc.)
3. Honing eye-hand coordination (throwing, catching).

Most first graders are not ready for hard-core competition, and most physical education teachers do not encourage that. Instead, games and activities are geared toward individual improvement, following simple rules, and having lots of fun. Your child may also begin learning about the basics of healthy living: staying fit, eating right, and avoiding drugs and alcohol.

Beyond Academics

As in kindergarten, teachers teach lots more than the three R's in first grade. Among the most important nonacademic subjects are:

- *Independence.* The time for babying your child is over. After the first week of school, teachers expect their students to walk into the classroom on their own. This may be harder for you than it is for your child. But it's important to encourage that budding independence. It's a crucial step toward independent learning.

- *Responsibility.* Like kindergartners, first graders spend a lot of time on self-management—learning, for instance, to hang up their own coats, tie their own shoes, pass in their lunch money, return books to the school library, write their name on their worksheets and tests, hand in assignments on time and in the right place, pick up after a project, and so on. These may seem minor to a parent, but they're major factors in making a classroom run smoothly, so that real learning can occur.

- *Organization.* This is the first year that many students have their own desks or lockers, have regular homework, and have to bring a lunch or lunch money to school. According to teachers, helping children remember what to do, and learn where to put things so they can find them when they need them, takes the better part of the school year.

Where It's All Leading

If your child's best friend is in a different school, or even a different classroom in the same school, and is learning different things, don't panic. For the most part, the specific facts, projects, and activities children do in all of the various subject areas are simply different ways of packaging and presenting the lifelong learning skills that schools are really out to teach. In first grade, these include the ability to:

- sit, listen, and learn
- ask questions—and find answers
- communicate ideas
- work independently
- take risks

- cooperate with others
- solve problems
- persist at a task until it's done
- be responsible for personal and work materials
- meet deadlines.

Most of all, first grade teachers want to spark a life-long love of learning.

Homework—and How to Help

Though some schools have a no-homework policy for first graders, most teachers do send home some kind of assignment two to four nights a week. There may be very little homework at the beginning of the year, and then more and more as skills and adjustment to first grade grow.

In general, teachers say, first grade homework should take anywhere from ten to twenty minutes to complete. And it shouldn't be too taxing. Its main purpose is to reinforce what's already been covered in the classroom.

Types of Homework

Different teachers send home different kinds of assignments, of course. But among the most typical for this grade are:

- *Spelling words*—a list of up to ten words that the child is expected to memorize for a test at the end of the week

- *Sight words*—flash cards with important words for the child to review, so he'll have an easier time with upcoming reading assignments

- *Phonics review*—worksheets or activities that drill the child in specific phonics skills

- *Math pages*—worksheets that echo math activities the child has done in class

- *Finish-up work*—work that the child was supposed to complete in school, but for one reason or another didn't

- *Special projects*—dioramas, reports, posters, or other special activities that require more than one night to prepare

- *Reading*—a book or story, either assigned by the teacher or chosen by the child, that must be read with the help of an adult.

As in kindergarten, reading with your child every night is considered the most important homework for this grade. In fact, most teachers recommend it whether it's assigned as official homework or not. "It is so important to keep reading with and to your child, even after he's learned to read by himself," stresses Doris Willmann of Lake Ridge Academy, in North Ridgeville, Ohio. "It not only helps build your child's vocabulary, comprehension, and listening skills, it encourages a love of literature, and boosts writing skills as well."

Parent Involvement

Most first grade teachers expect parents to be involved in homework. The best way to help is to:

- Agree on a time for your child to do the homework. It could be right after school, after your child has had a chance to play a while, after an afternoon snack, after supper, or before bedtime—whatever works best for you and your child.

- Sit with your child and ask her what she thinks she's supposed to do. If she's not sure, say, "Let's read the directions together."

- Once your child understands the directions, let her know that you'll stay nearby to answer questions, but that she has to do the work herself.

- Once she's finished, check her work over. If you notice a mistake, don't just give her the correct answer. Put a check near the problem and encourage her to try it again. If she still gets it wrong, work it out *with* her, not for her. If the material seems to be way over your child's head, leave the mistake alone and send a note to the teacher. Your child may need extra help learning something, or easier homework.

- When the homework is done, tell your child to put it in her backpack right away, so it won't get left behind when she leaves for school.

Measuring Progress

This may be the year your child first gets an official report card. But chances are, it won't look like the report card you got in first grade. It will probably be more detailed.

For example, my son Gus's first grade report card

included eleven overall categories: Reading, Social Studies, Writing, Science, Mathematics, Health, Social Skills and Work Habits, Speaking and Listening Behavior, Music, Art, and Physical Education. Each category included a checklist with anywhere from two to twenty-two subheads. Under "Reading," for instance, there were nineteen different subheads, including:

- Listens and responds to literature
- Sees self as a reader
- Knows letter sounds
- Is developing a sight word vocabulary
- Retells main idea of text; sequences events
- Understands basic punctuation
- Discusses plot, character, events, and setting
- Reads independently for extended periods
- Makes appropriate book choices.

For each of the subheads, my son was given either an *I* (for "does it independently"); a *W* (for "does it with help"), or an *NY* (for "not yet"). He was never ranked or evaluated in terms of how he was doing compared to his classmates. Instead, there were four marking periods, so I could see where he was making progress at regular intervals throughout the year.

Beyond the Report Card

My son's teacher didn't stop at writing up the report card. She scheduled a parent/teacher conference each time a report card was issued, to show me samples of my child's work and answer any questions I might have. She also sent home a written evaluation at the end of the year.

Teachers say it takes more time to do this kind of evaluation, but it's worth the effort. "Parents still really hang on to grades," says Barbara Maughmer of Amanda Arnold Elementary School in Manhattan, Kansas, "because it's the only thing they know. But grades can be deceptive and may provide a false sense of security." For example, if your child gets perfect scores on all of her reading worksheets, you might think, "Wow. She must be a really good reader." But reading off a worksheet and understanding a book are not the same thing. And some children who can do one easily can't do the other until they get further along in development. A simple grade won't tell you that.

Learning from Mistakes

Another way teachers measure progress today is by having students evaluate themselves. One method is by using rubrics, or prompts, to define assignments. For example, the teacher might write on the board: Pretend you have a new pen pal who lives in another state. He wants to know all about your school. Write him a letter that includes:

- the name of your teacher
- the number of students in your class
- the two subjects you like best.

When the child is finished with the assignment, he can check the list to see if he included all of the information he was supposed to. This teaches him to focus on and follow directions and helps him evaluate his own performance. Sometimes, teachers will even let the kids determine their own rubrics for an assignment.

In other classrooms, children are periodically asked to rate themselves on various behaviors, such as raising a hand instead of blurting out an answer; turning homework in on time; and following directions. By comparing their current answers to their previous ones, they can see for themselves where and how they're progressing.

What to Expect on the Social Scene

As important as they are, academics are far from being the main focus of first grade. Teachers spend a great deal of time and energy this school year on helping children become independent, self-reliant, and responsible. And social skills are taught practically around-the-clock.

"Will I Have a Friend?"

"When my son Hugh started first grade, his biggest— maybe only—concern was: 'Will any of my friends from kindergarten be in my class?'" says Holly Hughes. "As soon as he found out that his best friend would be there, he couldn't wait to go to school."

That's how most children feel. In fact, having friends is so important that the words most first graders dread more than anything are "You're not my friend." They think that's the worst phrase in the world—even if they can't stand the person who's saying it.

The plus side of actively wanting friends is that your child may be more willing than ever to share, cooperate, or compromise in order to make and keep them. As one teacher observes, "I've seen kids offer to give up their dessert at lunch just to get invited to a birthday party." But the downside is that friendships still tend to be quite fluid in this grade, and your child may end up spending most of her emotional energy on staying socially afloat.

Friendships in Flux

Although some first graders are able to form lasting bonds with one or two peers, most flit from friend to friend as their interests and circumstances shift. Anything from sitting together on the bus to liking the same action figures or having the same dessert for lunch can initiate a bond. And anything from sitting next to a different child or finding someone else who likes Oreos in her lunch box, can dissolve it in a second.

Even though this is the norm, it never ceases to upset kids. They expect their friendships to last forever. And the minute a new friend starts being friendly to someone else, they feel devastated and betrayed.

So don't be too surprised if your child comes home one day complaining "Nobody likes me" or "I have no friends." It's probably not true. "The first time I heard my daughter, Rita, say that in first grade it just broke my heart," says Denise Bullwinkel. "I felt bad for her, and I was worried. I didn't know what to do, so I started talking to other mothers—and I found out that all of their kids were saying the same thing. I talked to the teacher, too, and she said it was perfectly normal for the grade. There are just a lot of social issues being worked out at this age."

The Meaner Side of Six

There's another factor that makes first grade friendships so volatile: Kids this age don't like playing second fiddle.

They all want to be the winner, the leader, the person in charge of all the toys. So even though they're willing to make some compromises to further a friendship, first graders will go only so far. And if they feel at all threatened, they'll strike out physically, verbally, or emotionally—even against their best friend.

As one teacher notes, "It's scary, sometimes, to see how cruel kids can be to one another. They'll use anything from teasing to name-calling, ignoring, ridiculing, or laughing to make another child upset." Though it's not universal, teachers add, girls tend to get more involved in verbal cross fire and hurt feelings than boys do; hitting and physical aggression are more common in the male realm.

When conflicts do arise, it's best to be supportive, without blaming or overreacting. In school, for example, teachers will often resolve conflicts by walking kids through the following three steps:

1. Tell the other child how you feel (for example, *"I'm really sad"*).
2. Tell her why you feel the way you do (*"You hurt my feelings when you said I was dumb"*).
3. Tell the other child what you want her to do (*"I want you to take it back"*).

Handling a Chronic Complaint

If your child comes home daily with complaints about being left out or teased by a classmate, or starts withdrawing or clamming up about school, don't hesitate to call the teacher. There may be something she can do in the classroom to smooth social interactions, encourage friendships, or discourage a bully. The teacher may also be able to tell you which children your child seems most interested in, so you can invite them home for play dates.

Of course, it may turn out that your child is behaving in a way that turns other children off. And the teacher might have some suggestions for improving your child's social interactions. If that's the case, try to remain open-minded. As one teacher notes, "If you refuse to believe your own child could ever be at fault, you're doing him a great injustice. All children are capable of misbehaving."

The After-School Schedule

Friendships will probably be a bigger consideration in your child's after-school routine, too. But, as in kindergarten, less is more when it comes to structured activities after school.

One or two afternoons with planned activities is plenty for most first graders. After a long day of school, the kids are tired; they need time to relax and unwind—and to be on their own for a while (especially at the beginning of the school year).

Even if your child insists that his energy is boundless, don't believe it. "My daughter would be busy every minute of the day if I let her do everything her friends are doing," says Denise Bullwinkel. "But I limit her outside activities to two a week (for example, Brownies and ice skating). Otherwise, she'd wear herself out and I'd have major meltdowns to contend with."

The Best Bets

The best way to balance out the school day in first grade

is to include some play dates, some playground time, and one or two other activities—such as Brownies, Cub Scouts, or an organized sport—in the weekly schedule. Anything that gets your child moving around is an especially good choice.

Kids this age are gaining better control of their bodies. Many are also getting interested in specific sports. But they aren't quite ready to follow strict rules. So don't jump into organized teams and leagues—unless they're extremely noncompetitive. First graders are very sensitive and tend to react badly when they lose at anything. So at this point, you're better off encouraging cooperation rather than competition.

Also, avoid any sport in which the risk of injury is high (such as football) or the training and workouts are strenuous. Children this age are growing rapidly and don't always know their own physical limits, so injuries to bones and muscles are a notable risk.

Less Structure, More Fun

If your child goes to a regular after-school care program, make sure it's relatively flexible and offers plenty of opportunities for physical movement and free play. The last thing a first grader needs after a full day of school is more time sitting in a chair doing pencil-and-paper work. She should be discovering her own ways to have a good time.

This is also an age when children need to be supervised, however. So make sure there is a responsible adult in charge of any after-school care your child receives.

If you could only use one word to describe second grade, it would have to be *plateau*. This is a year when students, teachers, and parents finally get a break from the long climb upward, from preschool to real school. Learning and growing don't stop this year, and social and behavioral problems don't just disappear. But it should begin to feel as though your child is moving along on more level terrain.

A GREATER SENSE OF CALM

Second grade is when most children hit their stride at school and begin to feel more settled and competent. You may even notice a difference on the very first day.

"Sending my twins off to second grade was so much easier than sending them to kindergarten and first grade," says Tamara Eberlein, a mother of three. "They weren't at all worried about leaving home, riding the bus, or getting around in the school—they were old hands at all that," she explains. "Instead, for the first time, they were actually excited to be going back and seeing their friends."

And they came home with a lot more energy, Eberlein adds. "First grade was a big adjustment for them, because it was their first full-day program," she explains. "By the time they got home from school they were all tired out. Now, in second grade, as soon as they get off the bus they're ready for the next activity, whether it's a computer or dance class, a play date, or a chance to run around the backyard."

"That's what I love most about second grade," adds Chris Burton, a father of two. "The kids are like old pros. They may have some initial jitters about getting a new teacher or making new friends, but it doesn't take them long to settle in. They've finally accepted the fact that if you're a kid, you go to school. And they're ready to make the most of it. My son, Peter," he adds, "doesn't even want me to walk him to the bus stop anymore."

LETTING GO

This growing independence may bring you a sense of relief. Or you may feel somewhat sad that your child no longer needs—or wants—you to kiss him good-bye at the bus stop or drop him off at the classroom door. You might even feel a tad resentful when he acts like he values his teacher's word over your own. But it's important to hide these feelings and support your child's deepening attachment to school. The more comfortable and committed he is to that environment, the more likely he is to succeed.

What Second Graders Are Like

They have the innocence and enthusiasm of first graders, but they're more mature, they have more self-control, and they're better at working independently.

Second graders are also a little less egocentric and a little more willing to consider other people's feelings and opinions. They're even starting to notice the nuances of interpersonal communication.

"One Sunday, after church, I invited a classmate of my son James over to play," says Tamara Eberlein. "The boy said yes, but he said it reluctantly, and the initial look on his face definitely said no. As we were walking away, my son said, 'You know, Mom, I don't think he really wants to come.' A year ago, James wouldn't have even noticed the boy's look, much less tried to interpret it."

Their Eyes Are Opening

Second graders are beginning to awaken to the wider world beyond home and school. They're starting to pick up more information through reading. They're becoming more attuned to the concept of cause and effect. And they're getting better at making connections between various bits of information.

In addition, they're curious, enthusiastic, and persistent. They love being talked to—and listened to. They ask lots of questions (especially "What does that mean?" and "What does this say?"), and they're beginning to draw their own conclusions.

In fact, you may find that your child is acquiring more definite likes and dislikes and growing more stubborn.

Second graders are grown-up enough not to do something just because you said to. They want *reasons*.

"My daughter, Emily, has definitely become more analytical this year," says Katy Musolino, a mother of two. "Now, when I ask her to do something like quit playing Nintendo, or hurry up and get dressed for school, she's quick to question why. I don't think she's trying to be defiant," adds Musolino. "She just really wants to know the reasons for things now. Sometimes, she gets so involved in analyzing a situation that she can't fall asleep at night; she just lies in her bed, quietly thinking things over."

Thinking and Worrying

Second graders don't just analyze more, they worry more, too—about anything and everything. If they hear about a bomb exploding on the other side of the world, for instance, they'll worry about their house being bombed. If they go on vacation, they'll worry about burglars stealing their toys. If a parent gets sick, or they get ill themselves, they'll worry about death.

Even simpler concerns—Who will pick me up from school? Who will sit next to me on the bus? Will the teacher like me? and What will my friends say if I wear that shirt?—can easily consume a second grader's time and attention.

Other big worry triggers include:

- *Trouble at home.* Anything from a sick sibling or an argument between parents to death, divorce, or financial troubles can distract a second grader from schoolwork.
- *Changes in routine.* Second graders don't like surprises. And they don't like change. So little things,

like getting a substitute teacher, having a change in the school schedule, meeting a new after-school caregiver, or rearranging furniture at home, can send their minds spinning.

- *Doubts about personal abilities.* Younger children tend to have overinflated ideas about what they can do. In second grade, they start becoming more accurate at gauging their own abilities, and more realistic when comparing themselves to their peers. But their standards tend to be high, and they usually strive for perfection—which means that anything less may lead to a tailspin.

Turning Inward

Though second graders tend to worry more than their younger schoolmates, it's often harder to tell when they're upset. There will, of course, be days when your child is so angry or frustrated that she threatens to quit school or run away from home. But more often than not, you'll see some form of nervous behavior or moping. Your child might chew on her clothes, for instance, or bite her nails, pull at her hair, or gaze off into space.

If you notice these kinds of behaviors, it's worthwhile to ask "Are you feeling okay today?" or "Is there something on your mind?" Sometimes your child will have a relatively harmless concern, such as "What if I miss my favorite TV show?" or "Will I be late for school?" Other times she might be pondering something she doesn't understand, like her math homework. But every now and then, your child will have a serious concern that you can help with.

Often, all a seven- or eight-year-old needs is reassurance that everything's going to be okay, or that even if a classmate called him a "dummy," he really isn't stupid. It also helps to remind him of the things he's good at: "You're a great reader"; "You really know how to get a job done"; "Look how much you've learned in math!" As one teacher puts it, "At this age, children still believe almost anything adults tell them, so reassurance can go a long way."

The Quest for Fairness

The only time reassurance won't help is in discussions about fairness. This is a big issue with second graders. They view anything they consider unfair as an intrusion of their own selves—and they aren't shy about saying so. Comments like "It's not fair! He got to walk over and get a drink, and I didn't" and "She got to be the leader last time" are practically part of the daily routine.

It's important to talk about fairness when the issue comes up. Ask your child: "Why don't you think it's fair?" and "What would be fair in this situation?" But don't go overboard in trying to accommodate your child's sense of fairness. For one thing, it might not be logical or applicable. For another, it won't help your child grow. The goal is to instill a sense of fairness—but not an expectation that life is always fair.

It also helps to keep rules to a minimum. Stick to those few points you feel are essential and be flexible about the rest. For instance, you might insist that your child make up her bed before school every morning, but let her decide whether to do it before breakfast or after.

With a second grader, setting too many rules only leads to nitpicking and tattling (as in, "Mom, Karen is

eating breakfast and she didn't make up her bed yet!")
and endless arguments about fairness ("No fair! She gets
to have breakfast and I have to make up the bed").

An Easier-Going Year

Aside from arguing and tattling, the most common
behavior problems teachers see in second grade are inat-
tention and impulsive behavior (such as calling out
answers, grabbing from a classmate, running down the
hallways, or playing with a pencil when the teacher is
speaking). "Children this age are still very lively, and
curious," notes Michele Manos of The Kew-Forest School.
"And they're so used to the pace of television, movies, and
video games, they don't always have the patience to wait
their turn or pay attention while others are talking. Also,
a lot of children today don't have as many opportunities
as children used to have, to just sit around with their
family and learn how to have a conversation. We spend a
lot of time in second grade developing those listening,
speaking, and waiting skills."

You should also be aware that second graders are not
the most organized creatures on earth. And they usually
have so much going on in their minds that they get easily
distracted and lose things. For instance, they'll complain
they can't find their pencil when it's sitting right in front
of them. Or they won't know their own clothing, even if
they just took it off their body. Plus, they always seem to
be losing lunch boxes, hats, and gloves.

The good news is, kids do a lot of growing up in second
grade, so it pays to be patient. By the end of the school
year, you'll see definite improvements in your child's
work habits, organization skills, and sociability.

What Second Graders Should Know

By now, the fundamentals of reading, writing, and arithmetic should already be in place. For instance, among other things, your child should be able to:

- *Read a simple book*—even if it has only a couple of words on every page. Since reading is so closely linked to development at this stage, teachers aren't overly concerned about *how well* a child is reading. But they do want to know that the child can read short sentences and can understand *why* she's learning about letters, letter sounds, and words. If your child is struggling with reading, don't despair. Second grade is when late bloomers tend to blossom.

- *Write a simple story.* The sentences may be quite basic, and the spelling may be way off. But your child should show some understanding of basic punctuation (you capitalize the first word of a sentence and put a period at the end, for instance), and have lots of confidence that he can put his thoughts onto paper.

- *Do some basic math.* That includes adding and subtracting through sums of twelve, solving one-step problems, and relating math to everyday life (with time, money, and measuring, for instance).

- *Follow simple directions.* A second grader should be able to hear or read a one- or two-step direction and follow it without outside help. For example: "Take out your spelling list so we can review it as a class" or

"Read each sentence and underline every word that describes a color."

You Still See Extremes

The above is a list of shoulds, and not musts, however. In second grade, children still show wide variations in development. Some can read at a fourth or fifth grade level; others can barely decode words. Some can do complicated sums in their heads, while others still need to count on their fingers.

Most teachers say that being ready to learn, and feeling confident you *can* learn, are still more important than academic achievement. And most would rather have a class full of children who've been read to and love books than any number of students who have advanced academic skills but hate reading, fear math, or lack the confidence or willingness to try new things.

Questions about readiness are most likely if a child is younger or smaller than his classmates and appears immature for his age. For instance, a teacher might be concerned about a child who, by the end of first grade:

- isn't showing an interest in becoming more independent in self-care routines and schoolwork
- isn't able to focus on a task until it's completed
- doesn't feel comfortable making simple choices
- needs lots of direction from the teacher to complete routine assignments.

But, again, most teachers will work with any child who enters their classroom.

What to Expect in the Classroom

In most schools, the second grade environment does not differ dramatically from the first grade design. Different teachers have different strengths and talents, of course, and those are often expressed in different ways in their classrooms. One might be an animal lover, for instance, and fill her room with living creatures; another might have a passion for literature and cover her walls with posters from popular children's books.

Some will arrange children's desks in clusters of four or more; others might place them in a semicircle or in long, attached rows. Some won't even use desks: They'll stick to small tables, where children can work easily in groups.

The Daily Schedule

No matter what the classroom looks like, your child's day will probably be divided into distinct periods, with specific subjects (reading, math, social studies, and so forth) stressed at different times of the day. Or, if the curriculum is highly integrated (every activity incorporates elements of reading, writing, and math, for instance), and students work mainly in learning centers, they'll probably be switching activities at predictable intervals (every thirty to forty minutes). There's also always a lunch break, and time is usually allotted for physical activity (outdoor recess and/or gym).

Most second graders learn the schedule quickly—and rely on it. Now that they've finally figured out how things work at school, they want to maintain control. As one teacher notes, "If I so much as change a morning lesson to the afternoon, my students fall into flux. They get a lot of security from knowing the schedule, and they need lots of preparation to adjust to a change."

Different schools have different schedules, of course, but most second grade teachers build in time for:

- *Getting settled.* The first half hour or so is for getting students into school mode. At the beginning of the year, the children learn a morning routine that might include hanging up their coats, putting their lunch money or lunch boxes in a special place, and turning in their homework from the night before. They may also have to mark themselves as present and attend to classroom jobs, such as feeding the guinea pig, watering the plants, or writing a story for the classroom newspaper. Or, they may be told to finish up work from the previous day, play quietly in a learning center, or read silently until everyone is settled.

  A similar routine was probably part of your child's kindergarten and first grade experiences, but this year he'll have to take it more seriously. There may even be penalties for forgetting—such as points off the homework if it isn't on the teacher's desk before the first-period bell rings.

  "There's definitely a lot less coddling in second grade," says Carolyn Davenport, a mother of two. "In my son Zach's classroom, the children are expected to arrive at school and know exactly what to do and where to put things without being reminded. The teacher takes this so seriously that if a child is having trouble remembering the morning routine, she mentions it on the report card."

  But don't worry: Most teachers build in a grace

period. "I call the first six weeks of school 'boot camp,' because that's when I teach the children how to follow classroom routines and how to be responsible for themselves, their belongings, and their learning endeavors," says Julie Ferriss, of Madison Avenue Elementary School, in Madison, Mississippi. "I also stress that by taking responsibility, they create a successful learning community. But once 'boot camp' is over, I expect fewer questions about daily routines, and more independence."

- *Planning the day.* Once everyone is settled, there's usually a class meeting to preview the school day. The morning gathering might take place on the floor, in a carpeted corner of the room, or while everyone is sitting attentively at their desks. And it usually follows a preset agenda. The class might discuss the date, the weather, the news, birthdays or other celebrations, projects planned for the day, imminent deadlines and tests, or any changes in the usual routine. There may also be time for children to share personal experiences (about a vacation, a book they read, a movie they saw, a bad dream they had, and so forth), treasures from home, or preassigned reports on current events and other subjects. For example, Ellen Knudson, of Victor Solheim Elementary School, in Bismarck, North Dakota, has a different child in her class act as a "contributing scientist" each day. The child can share anything of a scientific nature that interests him or her—from a rock collection to a recycling project learned about on the Internet.

Getting children to feel comfortable speaking in front of peers is an important goal in second grade. It not only builds verbal skills, it adds to confidence and self-esteem.

- *Learning as a group.* There's always some time set aside for the teacher to introduce new information, or new ways to use existing skills, to the entire group. She might review some basic grammar rules, for instance, or explain the hypothesis behind an upcoming science project. She might read a book to the class or with the class, talk about the significance of an upcoming holiday, review spelling words, or explain various ways to solve math problems.

  In today's classrooms, however, you're not likely to see a teacher standing in front of the class lecturing for long periods. It's far more typical to see the teacher acting as a facilitator: someone who gives the children the basic tools and guidance they need to strike out and explore, discover, and learn on their own.

  This often includes following the children's lead, rather than rigidly sticking to a lesson plan. "Sometimes, you have to put aside planned lessons because a real-life issue comes up and the children want or need to talk about it," notes teacher Michele Manos. "For example, one day in my class we were talking about upcoming elections, and a Muslim child expressed surprise that I was planning to vote, because in the country his parents are from, women aren't allowed to. The resulting discussion turned into a lesson itself."

- *Meeting with the teacher.* In addition to providing group instruction, most teachers schedule regular "conference" times when they can sit with individuals, or small groups, and sharpen specific skills. While the class is busy with silent reading or writing, for instance, the teacher might meet with a child to explain corrections on a recent test or writing project or give a mini-lesson on reading strategies or punctuation. Children who are working ahead of their peers might receive lessons in advanced skills or be challenged by the teacher to tackle a special assignment.

- *Working with partners.* Cooperative learning is a bigger focus in today's classrooms than most parents will remember.

  Children not only read together, they work on math problems, science experiments, social studies projects, and art and music activities with partners or in small groups. In many classrooms, they even take tests together.

  Research shows that working in small groups helps children develop a lot of important life skills, such as how to listen, negotiate, compromise, and cooperate.

- *Working independently.* When children first start second grade, they're still babies in terms of their work habits. They need a lot of direction and involvement from the teacher. The goal, however, is to get them to the point where they can follow a multistep assignment on their own, or in a small group, without going back to the teacher every two minutes with a question.

  Most teachers start out slowly, giving one or two independent assignments a day. But by the end of the school year, they might hand their students a menu of twelve to fifteen tasks that they need to complete by the end of the week.

Children are also encouraged to do some silent reading and sustained writing every day. In September, it might be for only ten minutes at a time; by March or April, however, second graders can often read (or write) for as long as twenty-five minutes on their own.

- *Attending special classes.* In addition to physical education, lessons in art, music, and sometimes even computer skills and foreign languages are integral parts of most second grade curriculums. Children either leave their regular classroom for special instruction in these subjects, or a teacher who specializes in these areas visits the students in their own classroom on a regular basis.

  Many schools also have reading, math, speech, and other specialists who provide extra help for children who need it, either within the classroom or outside it. If the teacher tells you your child needs to work with a specialist, try to remain upbeat and supportive. It doesn't mean your child is the slowest kid in the class or is doomed to academic failure. It's more likely that she simply needs a little extra attention to get her over a learning hump.

- *Preparing to go home.* Like the morning meeting time, the last period of the day usually includes a group gathering. Children review the day and make sure they've put everything in its place, they know what their homework is, and they've packed up their backpacks. They may also have time to share what they learned, talk about what they liked or didn't like that day, and plan for the next day's activities.

Children today are much more involved in class-room management than we parents ever were. If a class has a bad day, for instance, the teacher might sit with the students during the last period and ask them why *they* think it happened. They might respond, "The work was too hard" or "We didn't have enough time to finish our math problems." And the teacher might tell them, "Next time you should let me know before you get frustrated." Together, they then come up with a plan to make the next day better.

The Learning Atmosphere

With a schedule like this, you can expect to see a lot of moving around and student-to-student interaction in your child's classroom. It may not be what you remember from second grade, but the looser environment is meant to encourage independent learning.

There's a big push in second grade to teach children that they can find answers to many questions by them-selves. When a child raises his hand to ask how a word is spelled, for instance, the teacher will now point him to the dictionary. If he wants to know what a snake's scales look like, she might hand him a magnifying glass and tell him to hold it up against the classroom snake's tank.

Sometimes, teachers will even pretend that they don't know an answer. "Hmm. I'm not really sure how to spell *tyrannosaurus*," a teacher might say, loudly enough for the whole class to hear. "I wonder how I could figure it out." That gives the children an opportunity to jump in with their own suggestions: "You could look in the dictio-nary"; "You could check that book about dinosaurs that we read this morning"; or even "Ask Ronnie—he knows how everything is spelled!"

The Most Important Subjects This Year

At this point, the three R's should be running neck and neck. Second graders need to gain strength in all of them—reading, writing, and arithmetic—so they can meet the greater learning demands of third grade. Here's a look at what to expect.

Reading

This is the year when most children move from being beginner readers to being competent, fluent, or advanced readers. And according to teachers, the progress a child makes this year can determine how he sees himself as a reader for the rest of his school life.

If a child isn't moving forward in reading, or can't read by now, he's going to have trouble in all the other subject areas.

It's also going to affect his frustration level and self-esteem. As one parent notes, "At the beginning of second grade, my son Mark felt so badly that his classmates could read and he couldn't that he started saying things like 'I'm so stupid' and 'I wish I were dead.' Even though he was doing really well in math and art, all he could think about was how he couldn't read."

Getting Up to Speed

The first reading-related goal of most second grade teachers is making sure that the children who are not yet strong readers catch up with their classmates. Whenever necessary, for instance, they'll take the time to work on phonics, rhyming patterns, word endings, and other basic reading strategies. Or, they'll arrange for special help, such as small-group reading instruction, partner reading, or one-on-one time with a tutor or reading specialist. Students also get lots of exposure to children's literature at whatever level they *can* read (regardless of what their classmates are reading).

In most cases, the little extra help can go a long way. "When my son Zach started second grade, he was reading—but not as fluently as many of his classmates," notes Carolyn Davenport. "I was very concerned, so I talked to the teacher, and she immediately hooked him up with the school's reading specialist. Within a few months, Zach was reading chapter books, just like his friends."

Watchful Waiting

The key, at this point, is to remain vigilant. Teachers say they watch students very closely during the first semester of second grade. But parents should be watchful, too. In particular, you want to look for signs that your child is feeling frustrated or turned off by reading. For example:

- Does he frequently complain that he hates to read, or that reading is "too hard" or "too boring"?
- Does he put himself down because his classmates are better readers than he is?
- Does he always seem to have something else to do when you invite him to sit with you and read a book?
- Does he read more slowly than other children his age?
- Does he frequently stumble over words that you've heard him read easily before?

- When he's finished reading a page or a story, does he have trouble answering questions about what he just read?

If the answer to any of these questions is yes, talk to your child's teacher. If the teacher doesn't seem concerned, find out why. It may be that she feels your child simply needs extra time to develop or more exposure to print-related experiences. But even if that's the case, you should ask for specific strategies you can use at home to build your child's reading skills.

If there is a physical or learning problem, the earlier it's diagnosed and addressed, the less likely it is that your child will feel bad or fall behind.

Building Comprehension

Once a child is reading fluently, the focus moves to building comprehension. While many children can read by now, they don't always have the concepts or vocabulary to understand the meaning of what they read. So something very simple—like not knowing what an "ear of corn" is—can throw a child off.

Teachers use a variety of strategies to build vocabulary. But they also expect parents to help—not by drilling a child on definitions to her spelling words, but by:

- *Exposing her to lots of different people and places— and talking about the experiences.* For instance, take your child to a local farm and point out what an ear of corn is, or show her a real fire station with a hook-and-ladder truck, or a hospital with an emergency room, or even a garden with a variety of different plants. Any time you can directly connect an object to a word, a child is more likely to remember and understand it. And the more exposure a child gets to different environments, people, and experiences, the more her vocabulary is going to grow.

That's why school field trips are so important. It's also why teachers spend so much time encouraging children to read—both at school and at home. More exposure to print means more exposure to new words—which leads to a larger vocabulary and greater comprehension.

- *Talking about specific words.* That's what teachers do in school. For instance, the teacher might take a word like *hut* and ask the children to come up with all of the criteria they can think of to describe what a hut is. Or she might ask them to tell her how a hut differs from a house. Other times they'll look at how words are related ("What's the link between *saber, light-saber,* and *saber-toothed tiger?*" or "Why do we see the word *cloth* in *clothes?*"). Second graders are fascinated by word relationships, so this is a good time to point them out.

Learning to Think

Another way teachers build comprehension is by asking probing questions about a story's content and concepts. For example: Who was the main character in this book? What was the main problem facing this character? How was the problem resolved? What was the setting of the book? If you changed the setting, how would the ending be different?

"It's not like the old days, when a child would read a passage and then answer five fact-related questions like 'What color was Mary's dress?'" notes one teacher. "Today we want the children to read and really think about what they're reading—and then be able to discuss it."

In school, children explore the "thinking" questions both verbally (through whole-class and small-group discussions) and in writing (through journals and workbooks). At home, you should casually work them in as you read books together.

Expanded Exposure

Another strategy is exposing children to different forms of print, including stories, poems, songs, recipes, newspaper and magazine articles, and even nonfiction books. In fact, a lot of reading groups today look more like research groups, because the students are reading nonfiction books on a science or social studies subject and then discussing it, or writing about what they learned.

The goal is to help students begin to view reading not as a skill but as a tool that can be used for different purposes. For example, you can read a piece of fiction for enjoyment, a book of jokes to have fun, a newspaper or magazine article to obtain information, or a letter to find out how a friend is feeling.

Writing

This is a breakthrough year in writing, partly because kids are more coordinated and can print more legibly, and partly because they're becoming better readers—and reading bolsters writing.

"It's fun to see how much growth there is in writing

from first grade to second," notes Tamara Eberlein. "In my twins' school, both grades have a writers' workshop where the children meet with parent volunteers once a week for forty-five minutes or so, to work on a piece of fiction or nonfiction. A lot of the children struggle with the writing in first grade," she adds. "But by second, you see amazing progress. The stories become longer (up from about two pages to an average of seven); the plots become more interesting and complex; and the characters become more developed (they have attributes, instead of just names). Some second graders really get into it," she adds, "and will write as many as twenty pages for their book."

All Writing Welcome

Most second graders aren't quite that prolific. But most second grade teachers do try to ensure that all of their students have lots of opportunities to write. And, as in first grade, the writing assignments tend to be varied. In addition to writing stories and reports, for example, your child may be keeping journals for different subject areas, communicating with a pen pal, writing a script for a class play, or producing copy for the classroom newspaper or literary journal. She may also be learning to use writing as a tool of persuasion and to use different senses (hearing, sight, smell, and so forth) to enhance her written descriptions.

Engaging children in different kinds of writing is important, teachers say, because it helps children learn that writing is more than just a school skill. It's a tool they can use for communication and self-expression in nearly all aspects of daily life.

A Slight Shift in Focus

The overall goal is still to help children feel comfortable putting their thoughts onto paper, but there's also more emphasis this year on structure and substance.

Children learn about what makes a good paragraph, for instance, and how to write a story with a beginning, a middle, and an end. Teachers also place more emphasis on revising and rewriting. Students will frequently do a first draft and a few revises before producing their final copy.

"In my daughter's classroom, they even do outlines," notes Thomas Mitchell, a father of three. "They call them story maps, but it's basically the same thing: They have to come up with their major points before they start writing. Then they do a first draft, which they review with their teacher—for grammar, spelling, punctuation, and even plot development. Then they write a final draft, which is supposed to be done in their very best penmanship."

In many cases, before the final draft is written, children also consult with their classmates, to get additional feedback on plot, characters, clarity, or even word choices. This not only helps with the revise process, it strengthens the students' oral communication skills.

The Writing / Spelling Connection

Teachers still don't want worries over spelling to slow a child down. So, often, they'll tell their students that if they don't know how to spell a word they can "invent" a spelling and underline the word. Then, when they're finished with their first draft, they can go back to the underlined words and find the correct spellings for the final draft. The goal is to teach children that writing is a multi-stage process, and while spelling is important, it's not the first concern.

But teachers also work on strengthening spelling skills in second grade. Your child may even get weekly spelling tests. Nowadays, however, the word lists often spring directly from books or topics the children are studying. For example, a unit on transportation might involve a spelling list with words such as *highway, airplane,* or *train.* In some classrooms, children maintain a notebook of words they're having trouble remembering, and there's a chart on the bulletin board that's regularly updated with common words the students should know.

"In my daughter Emily's classroom, the children have individual spelling lists, and they're taught to follow a specific routine when memorizing their words," notes Katy Musolino. "First they copy a word from their list. Then they cover it up and try to write it correctly from memory. They check to make sure they got it right, and then they repeat the process until they feel comfortable with that word. Then they move on to the next word. Once a week, they get together with a spelling partner and test each other on their word lists."

Looking At Words

Research shows that memorizing word lists won't turn a poor speller into a good one. So many teachers also build their students' visual memory for words by having them identify patterns and relationships within words. For example, they look at how vowel sounds change in words with different prefixes and suffixes and how words can be combined to create compound words. They also have children write a lot, so they can see their own spelling mistakes corrected.

Parents can help, teachers say, but not by being overly concerned about perfect spelling. "Parents need to remember that being a good speller is not easy when a child is in the throes of creativity," says Jean LaGrone of Westgate Elementary School, in Omaha, Nebraska. If your child is still bringing home stories with a lot of words misspelled, don't blow up. Try to enjoy what your child has written instead of criticizing his spelling. Later on, once you've praised his creativity, you can casually ask, "Would you like me to help you with your spelling?" or "I see a few words that need help with spelling. Would you like me to point them out?" But don't push too hard, or you may wilt his enthusiasm for writing.

The Role of Penmanship

You should expect your child's ability to form letters, write within the lines on a paper, and space words correctly to significantly improve this year, especially when it comes to producing a final draft in a writing project (though some teachers allow the final draft to be done on a computer). If there's no progress in this area, the teacher may recommend an evaluation, to see if there's a developmental or other problem holding your child back.

In some second grades, cursive writing is introduced toward the end of the year. But there's no big push to use it. At this point, it's mainly to familiarize the children with the kind of writing they'll be doing in third grade. Most children still need time to strengthen their hand muscles before cursive writing can become routine.

Math

As with reading and writing, the emphasis in math is on mastery. Second grade is when students are expected to get solid on addition and subtraction, so that regrouping (borrowing and carrying) and multiplication can begin.

While manipulatives still play a major role at this point, many second grade teachers also encourage memorization of math facts. So you can expect to see more math worksheets in second grade, and more math tests. "Every week, in my son Peter's class, they have a timed math test," notes Chris Burton. "The kids are given a sheet of maybe fifty addition or subtraction problems and told to do as many as they can within a certain amount of time. They then get certificates for reaching different levels of achievement."

Striking a Balance

There's no denying that memorizing math facts can improve a child's speed in adding and subtracting. But, according to today's thinking, it reflects a lower level of functioning. The higher level teachers are now striving for getting students to think mathematically, so they can apply what they learn to solving problems in their everyday lives.

In fact, many teachers design math problems around subjects that arise naturally in the classroom. For instance, when one class was reading a book about a woman who wanted to buy a comfortable chair, the teacher went out and found four ads for comfortable-looking chairs in the local newspaper. She then broke the class into groups and asked each group to figure out how many ten-dollar bills they'd need to buy the chair they wanted and to document their strategy for finding their answer. Because of the book, the students got excited about the math.

The Same, Except More

If you're worried that your child forgot how to add and subtract over the summer, you'll be happy to know that most teachers spend the first month or so of second grade on review work. They know that with young children a lot of knowledge gets lost over the summer. Also, they want to make sure the students really understand their basic math facts, so they can move on to place values and double- and triple-digit addition and subtraction.

As the year goes by, time and money are studied closely. And, as in first grade, there are lots of opportunities to practice estimating, measuring, graphing, and problem solving.

Many teachers also work math into class projects and activities. For example, for Valentine's Day, Julie Ferriss has her class run an in-school post office. The children design their own stamps, including a one-cent stamp for in-class deliveries; a ten-cent stamp for in-school deliveries; and a twenty-five-cent stamp for outside deliveries. They then take turns running their post office booth, selling the stamps, making the correct change, and delivering the mail. They donate any money they raise to the local heart association. "But more importantly," says Ferriss, "they learn a whole lot about math."

Even little everyday things, like having children keep track of the date, tally the lunch money, tell time, graph the class's daily attendance, and weigh and measure themselves regularly, make math more meaningful and less intimidating, teachers say.

Looking for Patterns

You may also notice that your child is spending a lot of time working with patterns. She may be using pattern blocks during math activities, searching for patterns during science and reading lessons, and playing pattern-related games.

For instance, during group time, the teacher might ask one student to create a sequence—such as clap/tap/stomp—and then have the others try to identify the pattern and copy it. Or, she might ask them to look for patterns on the calendar by circling all the dates with a five or a zero in them, or all the odd numbers versus all the even numbers.

These activities may look simple but, according to teachers, they get children in the habit of looking for patterns—and that helps with math. In fact, being able to see the regularity in something, and extrapolate the pattern into the future, is what advanced math (such as algebra and calculus) is all about.

Other Important Subjects

As in first grade, science and social studies themes vary from classroom to classroom. In general, however, the focus in *science* is still on teaching children to think like scientists. Students might be given a problem—such as "How many pennies (versus other objects) would it take to sink this plastic boat?"—and then be asked to formulate a hypothesis. They then set up the experiment, record the data, evaluate the results, and prepare written and oral conclusions.

There may also be flora and fauna in the classroom for the children to tend to and observe, visiting scientists, field trips to museums and other scientific sites, and nonfiction reading material available on classroom shelves. Among the most popular second grade science themes are: the environment, plants, animals, weather, the human body, and recycling.

In *social studies,* second graders begin to look at the bigger picture: people and places outside their own community. Map skills are stressed, as are the attributes of tolerance and respect for people who have different backgrounds and beliefs. (A growing number of schools even have an official "values" curriculum designed to promote sharing, respect, honesty, perseverance, and other civilized behaviors.)

Children read nonfiction books for social studies, write reports, and do special projects, such as dioramas, to demonstrate what they've learned.

Art, music, and *physical education* should also play distinct roles in your child's second grade education, and many schools offer additional instruction in *computer* use and/or a *foreign language.* Your child's teacher should be able to tell you what the specific curriculum goals are for each of these areas. If these subjects are not covered to your satisfaction in school (due to lack of equipment, insufficient teacher training, budget cuts, or overcrowded classes), you should work them into your child's after-school life. While not required for academic achievement, they all make invaluable contributions to learning, thinking, development, and self-esteem.

Homework—and How to Help

In some schools, homework is still not a big priority. It may consist mainly of an edict for the child to read something every night—preferably with or to a parent—and an occasional worksheet or research project.

"I don't give a lot of homework because most of my students have busy after-school schedules," says Charlotte Schumacher, of Lake Ridge Academy. "Some don't get home until seven P.M. Or, their parents aren't home until late and don't have time to help with the homework, so I try not to place that extra burden on the family."

In other schools, second grade is when homework starts getting serious. It may take an average of twenty to thirty minutes a night (though some teachers give even more after the middle of the school year). There may be:

- worksheets for math and language arts
- lists of spelling words that need to be put into sentences and memorized for tests
- books that need to be read and reported on
- writing assignments that range from keeping a journal to drafting a report.

Some second grade teachers also require one or two long-term projects (with written, oral, and hands-on components) during the year. For instance, children might be given three weeks to read a book, write a book report, and make a puppet, doll, or life-size drawing of their favorite character from the book. Then they give an oral presentation to their classmates.

The Parent's Role

If this is your first encounter with serious homework, prepare to have mixed feelings about it. As one father notes, "My daughter gets a pretty good dose of homework four nights a week. I know it's helpful for her, but I never realized how time-consuming her homework would be for me!"

Like it or not, you need to be involved. While second

graders are often responsible for writing their assignments in a special notebook, they're also prone to forgetting and losing things. Most of them need help getting the homework habit down.

That includes deciding when and where to get it done. Although some teachers stress the importance of setting a daily time for homework, others encourage any flexibility that enables the parent and child to work together.

Being There

Once your child has started her homework, your job is to stay nearby—and prepare to field lots of questions. Second graders have a habit of asking how to do things they already know how to do. As one parent notes, "My son gets really upset whenever he can't understand a direction or figure out an answer. But all he seems to need is to hear me explain it, and then he usually calms down."

So try to be patient. Give your child whatever help he asks for, but don't do the work for him. And don't get into fights over it. If your child can't calm down, or can't get his work done within a reasonable time, talk to his teacher. Homework is not so academically important at this point that it's worth fighting over.

When the Homework Is Done

Review the homework for errors and readability—but don't change any answers. Instead, point out problems that need to be redone, or help your child discover his mistakes by asking open-ended questions like "How did you find this answer?" or "Can you tell me why you think this answer is right?" If he still can't correct it, leave it alone so the teacher will know what your child has or hasn't learned.

Even if your child's homework is perfect, it doesn't hurt to ask a few questions. Having your child articulate why a certain answer is right or how she knows it's correct helps her internalize what she's learning.

Last but not least, remind your child to put her homework into her backpack—so it will actually make it back to school the next day. (Then you can only *hope* that your child will remember to take it out of the backpack and turn it in!)

Measuring Progress

By now, you should be familiar with the type of grading system used in your child's school. It may be a letter (or number) system or involve a combination of written evaluations, portfolio reviews, and parent/teacher conferences. Whichever approach is used, teachers say, it's important to maintain a big-picture perspective. One bad grade, or a less-than-glowing assessment in one or more subject area, only tells you so much about your child. And even good grades can be deceptive.

As one teacher notes, "Even though my school requires letter grades, I'm reluctant to give them to second graders. An A or a B (or a 1 or a 2, or even a check or check-plus) may demonstrate that a child has mastered a specific skill. But it can't tell you whether the child knows how to apply that skill in real-life situations; nor can it tell you how your child feels about learning, or reading, or doing math. Plus, it doesn't give you a feel for social skills and other nonacademic strengths."

"Bad grades don't help much either," she stresses. "If I

give a seven-year-old an F in math, it's just going to make the child feel bad. I'd rather say, 'This is what you can do, and this is what we need to work on.'"

How Teachers Grade

Even if your child's report card looks more like a developmental checklist than a roster of grades, it's important to remember that different teachers use different criteria for evaluations. These may include:

- how the student compares to others in his class
- how he compares to others in his age category
- whether or not he's achieved a specific preset goal
- how his own current work compares to his earlier work.

In the end, all grades and comments about a child are basically subjective. So you shouldn't view the teacher's word as the final say on your child's abilities or potential to succeed. If you have any questions about your child's report card or evaluations, or if you feel confused about the teacher's grading system, you should schedule a conference to discuss it.

About the only question on this subject that a teacher won't welcome is "How is my child doing compared to the rest of the class?" The most relevant questions are "Is *my child* moving forward?" and "Does she *enjoy* learning and going to school?" Not "Is she as smart as her classmates?"

Don't Add Pressure

Even if they don't show it, doing well in school is really important to second graders. School is a big part of their lives now, and they want to feel successful at it. If a child thinks she isn't doing well—whether it's true or not—it's going to affect her confidence and self-esteem.

So try to be positive—and focus on learning rather than achievement.

If Progress Is Lacking

If your child doesn't show the kind of progress his teacher desires, you should expect to hear about it before report cards are issued. The teacher may recommend extra help or tutoring, and will probably enlist your aid in building basic skills.

Toward the end of the school year, lack of progress— particularly in reading and math—might prompt the teacher to suggest your child be tested for learning or other problems. She should be able to describe the specific areas in which your child is not progressing and explain what the tests will consist of and how the results will be used.

"Parents react in different ways when teachers suggest testing," according to Cheryl Reardon, a basic skills coordinator at Constable Elementary School, in South Brunswick, New Jersey. "Some actually feel relieved, because they know their child is having problems and they want to do anything they can to solve them. Others will refuse the testing because they're afraid their child will acquire a negative label that will stick with her for the rest of her school life."

The most important thing, however, is not to take anything school professionals say about your child personally. "Listen to what the school has to say, compare it to what you know about your child's strengths and weaknesses, and make the decision you honestly feel is best for your child," Reardon advises.

If Your Child Seems Gifted

In many school systems, special educational programs for children who are "gifted" begin in the third grade. (Some schools start them earlier, some later, and some don't have them at all.) If your school has such a program, and you suspect your child would qualify, talk to her teacher in the spring of second grade and request the necessary testing. (For more on helping children who are gifted or advanced, see chapter 8.)

What to Expect on the Social Scene

This should be a calmer year. There's a lot less blaming and tattling in second grade. Kids tend to be more tolerant of each other and more willing to give up territory in order to get along. Boys and girls still play well together, and they aren't embarrassed to attend each other's birthday parties—yet. But as the year goes by, you may see more of a division of genders on the playground.

Relationships are still shifting and changing. And children are very sensitive. They'll get extremely upset if someone bumps them in a line, calls them a name, grabs a pencil out of their hands, or laughs at something they say, for instance. And they're often devastated when they lose a best friend. Second grade teachers say they spend as much time ironing out social wrinkles as they do teaching reading, writing, and math.

Superficial Friendships

Second grade friendships are usually based on the need of the moment—as in "You're my reading partner today, so let's be best friends." There isn't as much physical or verbal fighting as in first grade, but you may see more excluding (for example, "You can play with me in the classroom but not on the playground"). The "two's company, three's a crowd" mentality persists, and you may hear about "secret clubs" with fairly exclusive membership requirements (as in "Girls with Long Hair Only" or "Boys Who Like Soccer Only").

Although group play is not terribly organized (second graders are just beginning to get good at following rules), most children want to be part of a group and will worry about their status amongst their peers. They also watch each other like hawks—to see who's breaking the rules and who's being fair or unfair.

Today's Complications

In some classrooms, minor altercations are exacerbated by the fact that the children come from very different home environments. "When I first began teaching, more than twenty years ago, most of the students in my class were from similar backgrounds," explains one teacher. "Now I have children who not only come from different types of families [for instance, single parent households, families in which both parents are working, and extended-family units], but also from very different religious, ethnic, and economic backgrounds. It's difficult, sometimes, to find common ground on which every child in the class can feel comfortable and respected."

But that's the goal most second grade teachers pursue—through constant communication, skill building, and daily interventions. With second graders, you need to address problems as soon as they arise, they say, because the children don't have a lot of long-term memory skills to rely on. And when a child's feelings are hurt, his mind is not open to learning.

If a teacher can't address a problem right away, she'll give a short-term response to hold the child until later, when she can discuss the situation in more depth.

Second grade teachers also spend time talking about things like how to cool down when you're angry and how to tell someone you're upset without starting another fight. And they know that most of what they say will have to be repeated over and over again. As one teacher notes, "Even when a child understands and accepts what you say about behavior during a class discussion, it doesn't mean she'll carry it over to her own behavior on the playground. Learning to respect others is a long process."

The Parent's Role

It's important to be sensitive to your second grader's friendship-related concerns. But don't go overboard and start worrying that your child's social life is a disaster. As one teacher notes, "Parents are always asking me, 'Does my child have any friends at school?' They hear their child complain so much that nobody likes him that they begin to worry that it's true. But in most cases, the answer is 'Yes, your child does have friends.' Or, if the answer is 'No,' it's usually because the child has chosen to play alone or doesn't yet feel a strong need for a best friend."

Some second graders don't have a lot of close friends, and it doesn't seem to bother them. So if your child seems happy and is able to get along with her classmates, there's no need to worry because she doesn't have an established circle or one best friend.

Sensitive Discipline

If your child gets into trouble for hurting someone else's feelings, try to avoid confrontational questions like "Why did you call Johnny a name on the playground?" By now, kids know better. And they're usually better at controlling their impulses, teachers say. But they're not perfect. They make mistakes and lose their cool just like everyone else. But now, instead of blaming, they're more apt to feel guilty—and they don't want to be reminded of their crime.

A better approach would be: "I heard you and Johnny had some trouble on the playground today. Want to talk about it?" Then, later, "What do you think you could do differently next time, so that won't happen again?"

The After-School Schedule

Don't be surprised if your child wants more say about after-school activities. Second graders are more aware of what they do well, and more definite about what they're interested in. This is a great time to give your child deeper exposure to something she really likes but doesn't get to do in school, such as dance, music, and art lessons, or computer, chess, swimming, or gymnastics. Positive outside experiences build self-esteem and give your child something special to talk about with her peers.

Group activities that foster cooperation and teamwork—such as Scouting or noncompetitive sports—are still great choices. Kids this age are ready and eager to gain experience working with others. They're even willing to lose a game now and then (though they may want to play that game over and over, until they finally win). But they aren't quite ready yet for the rigors of head-to-head competition.

Keep It Light

Try not to overdo it. Second graders may seem more energetic and competent, but their bodies are still young and growing, and they need lots of rest. If they're up too late at night because of overscheduling, they can't hang in at school.

"I see some children coming into my classroom who are so exhausted by their after-school schedule that they look like death warmed over," says one teacher. "I see others whose parents are pushing them so hard to be the best at something that they don't have any time to just run around and have fun." And then there are the children who come in and say, "I couldn't do my homework because I had a soccer game last night."

"Kids this age don't need a different after-school activity every night of the week," adds Debbie Maxa, a teacher at the Philip R. Smith School, in South Windsor, Connecticut. "They need downtime—moments when they can daydream or dabble, or find their own fun."

Time Alone

Second graders also need time alone and privacy. As one parent notes, "Second grade was the first year that my son would come home from school and disappear in his room, instead of asking to play with friends. At first I thought he was having trouble at school. But every time I'd ask him, he'd say, 'I just want some privacy.'"

This isn't unusual. By second grade, most children are in the process of discovering who they are. They need a special place to retreat to, where they can sit and think about their likes and dislikes and their feelings and opinions. Or, they may just want some peace and quiet so they can daydream, write in their diary, play alone with their Legos, play left hand against right hand in a board game, or tend to their private collection of rocks, stamps, or baseball cards.

Let your child have this time. He doesn't always have to be an achiever: He also needs time just to be a kid.

*P*repare for another leap year. Not in terms of the calendar, but in terms of what your child will be doing in school. Third grade marks another big transition time, when children are moving upward as well as forward.

The primary school period is ending, and the intermediate years are about to begin. So nearly everything about third grade involves growing up. This is the year when most children begin to switch from learning to read to reading to learn. It's when homework, tests, and grades become inescapable realities. And it's the beginning of the end of when children prefer their parents over peers.

A TOUGHER YEAR

There's no question that third grade will be harder for your child than second grade. But it may also be the best year yet. As Pam Allen, a mother of three, notes, "Third grade is when everything came together for my daughter, Emily. She became fluent in reading, her writing became more creative and complex, and she was able to move into more advanced math. She also became more confident and outgoing. It's as though all the seeds that were planted in first and second grade finally began to blossom."

What Third Graders Are Like

Most of the time, they're a pleasure to be with. This is an age when many children catch up with themselves. Their cognitive, social, and emotional development begin to even out; their more refined physical abilities give them greater independence; and their growing desire to converse on subjects other than themselves makes them fairly pleasant companions.

In fact, in many ways, third graders pull together the best of both primary and intermediate school students. For example:

- *Like first and second graders,* they're still curious, enthusiastic, and eager to learn. And it doesn't take much to motivate them. "By fifth grade, the kids will sit at their desks with their arms folded and give you a 'Go ahead and try to teach me something' stare," explains Sharon Smith, a teacher at Dry Creek School, in Rio Linda, California. "But in third grade, the children still really *want* to learn. And they still look to adults for inspiration." So you see a lot of energy and enthusiasm in the classroom.

What's also great is that most third graders aren't

yet too self-conscious to ask a question, venture an answer out loud, or try something new. In fact, many teachers say that what they love most about kids in this grade is that they're open, honest, and innocent. And they still enjoy it when the teacher does something unexpected—like sing a silly song about numbers, make up rhymes to reinforce rules, or even wear the costume of a book character or historical figure to school.

Another plus from the primary years is that you still see a lot of teamwork and cooperation in third grade. At school, a mere mention that the teacher could use some help (passing out papers, cleaning up art materials, or erasing the blackboard) results in a chorus of "Let me do it! Please!" (Of course, that may not happen as often or as easily at home.) And third graders are still fairly accepting and supportive of their classmates. They might start to tease each other, but they'll usually listen (and immediately feel guilty) if an adult tells them to stop.

- *Like fourth and fifth graders,* third graders are more mature, competent, and confident than their younger schoolmates. "Children make a big leap in third grade," notes George Burns, head of the middle school at the Bank Street School for Children in New York City. "There is a marked difference in their studious-ness. They've already mastered the basics; they're getting much better at articulating ideas; and while they still need a lot of hands-on exposure, they can now draw on past experiences when learning new things."

Most of all, they don't want to be babied anymore.

They want to pick out their own clothes, get their own snacks and drinks, choose their own lunches, and decide when to do their homework. They want you to trust them to walk over to a friend's house, choose their own TV shows, or ride a bike alone down the street. And when it comes to after-school activities and play dates with friends, they mainly want you to drive them, pick them up, and let them be.

You can't always let your third grader do exactly what he wants, of course. Sometimes an eight- or nine-year-old's desire for independence exceeds his maturity—or your sense of safety. But the fact that your child is seeking more autonomy is a good sign that he's growing up.

More Good Signs

In addition to being more independent, many children in this grade are more outgoing. Put a third grader in a group of younger kids, for instance, and you'll soon see the eight-year-old taking over and organizing a game. Introduce her to someone new, and instead of hiding her face or leaning into your legs, she might actually look up and say something polite, like, "Hi. I'm Paula. I'm eight."

After all their analyzing and internalizing in second grade, most eight- and nine-year-olds are ready to reach out and take in new knowledge, new friends, and new experiences. It's as though they've finally realized that they're not the *only* interesting subject in the world. And they've decided they want to know more.

To teachers, the difference is significant. "With second graders, in the middle of a lesson on weather, someone might raise their hand to tell you what they did with their Uncle Henry that weekend," explains Ed Silver, a teacher at Millington Elementary School, in Millington, Maryland. "Third graders will raise their hands to ask real questions, like, 'Why *does* it sleet sometimes, and snow other times?' or 'How *can* the weather person tell it's going to rain?'"

And they're far more persistent with their questions. For instance, if you tell a second grader that a music or dance class has been canceled, the child will want to know why. But all you have to say is "Your teacher is sick." A third grader will want to know more: What's wrong with the teacher? How'd he get that illness? Is it contagious? Will he have to take medicine? When will he get better? and so on.

Older—But Not Grown Up

When things are going well with a third grader, it can seem like heaven. As Daniel Cunningham, a father of two, notes, "It's so much more fun to spend time with my son now. We're not just talking about cartoons and action figures anymore. He's also interested in the things I like—like baseball, and music, and even history."

Third graders can do more things, too, like actually play baseball, or make a musical instrument produce lovely music. They have their own opinions, and they aren't afraid to voice them. They're even starting to look more grown-up. Their bodies (and their appetites) are growing rapidly, and many are beginning to trade that willow-thin look of childhood for the curves and bulk of preadolescence.

It's important to remember, however, that no matter how grown-up your third grader looks or seems, she's still a child. Just because she nods her head and acts like she knows what you're talking about, it doesn't always means that she does. And just because she behaves better in public, it doesn't mean she's immune to getting cranky and defiant when she's tired, hungry, or stressed at home.

Even the most sophisticated third graders still like to play with toys and sneak their toys to school. And a surprising number will still cuddle a doll or stuffed animal, or suck on a thumb, when it's time to relax or go to sleep. "Despite all her airs of independence," says one mother, "my third grader is very much a little girl. She still loves to play with her dolls and ride back and forth on the swings in our backyard. And she still comes to me crying when her feelings are hurt or she scrapes her knee."

"My son is like two different people," adds a father. "By day he acts so grown up and mature, but at night he still sucks his thumb and sleeps with his favorite (stuffed) kitty."

Responding with Love

You may be tempted to come down hard on your third grader's more childish behaviors. But comments like "Stop acting like a baby" and "You're too old for that" won't help. For one thing, your child may be feeling so overwhelmed by the changes and demands of being more grown-up that he needs to regress a bit—and that's okay. After all, he's still a child.

Also, third graders tend to be extremely sensitive to criticism. They're growing more aware of their own strengths and weaknesses, but they don't have much perspective yet. So one critical comment can make them feel like *everything* they do is wrong.

They're also more aware, by now, of what the "good" and "bad" behaviors are. And most (even if they don't show it) are trying hard to be "good." What *they* don't realize—but parents should—is that it's impossible for any child to be good all the time.

So instead of attempting to shame your child into better behaviors, ignore the negative as much as you can (mainly the minor, annoying, or infrequent regressions) and praise the positive. Like most young children, third graders are suckers for positive reinforcement. "If I have to say something negative to a child, I always try to do it in a positive way," says teacher Karen Gunther, of the Kew-Forest School. "For example, instead of saying 'Your handwriting is a mess,' I'll say 'Try holding the pencil this way and the paper that way.' Then the child doesn't feel so threatened and is more willing to take a risk and try something new."

Praising accomplishments is also effective. But you can't go overboard. Third graders aren't easily convinced by statements like "You're the best kid in the whole world" or "I've never seen anyone draw as well as you do!" They know better. Instead, give specific, realistic praise: "Congratulations! You worked hard on that report and you got a great grade" or "That was very generous of you to share your gum with your sister."

Why Rules Help, Too

Being very specific about rules and consequences will also help. Most third graders actually welcome rules (as long as they're fair and there aren't too many of them). This is partly because they're finally getting good at remembering and following rules. But it's also because they're not always sure of their boundaries. Rules help them monitor and regulate their own behavior.

That's why many teachers spend a lot of time in the beginning of the school year establishing the exact procedures for everything from going to the water fountain and getting a drink to passing in homework and walking to the playground for recess. But the key, they say, is to get the child's input. Children this age not only have some pretty good ideas of what rules and consequences should be, they're also more able and willing to listen to reason. If you can convince a third grader that a rule is fair, he'll do his best to follow it.

What Third Graders Should Know

Teachers expect a lot more of third graders, in terms of both behavior and academics. So it will definitely help if your child starts the year with:

- *Good listening skills.* That includes the ability to focus when the teacher is explaining a lesson, reading a book, giving an assignment, or writing on the blackboard. There's less hand-holding in third grade and a lot more independent work. Children who have trouble listening and concentrating may have a hard time keeping up.

- *A sense of responsibility.* By third grade, teachers expect children to fall into daily routines quickly and to come to class prepared to work (with pencils, papers, books, notebooks, and other materials). Also, they're less forgiving when it comes to things like unfinished class work, missing homework, and lost books.

- *A strong grasp of addition and subtraction.* Your child should also have a solid sense of numbers (knowing what "4 + 4" means, for instance) and the ability to use different strategies (such as drawing a picture, counting out objects, or creating a graph) when solving word problems. Exposure to the multiplication tables up to ten or twelve is useful, since that's a major focus in third grade.

- *A desire to read for pleasure.* The ideal is a child who can read grade-level books fluently, understand and remember the material she reads, and figure out unfamiliar words using a variety of strategies. But even if reading is not your child's strongest subject, she should at least show that she enjoys reading when a book is enticing.

- *The ability to write simple sentences.* Not just "I am a girl" or "I like cats," but something like "I like to go to school because I get to learn math." It'll also help if your child can group four or five sentences into a paragraph and can tell the difference between a topic sentence and a supporting one.

- *An awareness of cursive handwriting.* Some schools introduce this as early as second grade, others as late as fourth. But most make the switch to writing (and reading) in cursive sometime during third grade. Proficiency isn't necessary yet, but familiarity will help.

If You Have Any Doubts

Not all eight- and nine-year-olds are at the same level at the start of third grade, so you shouldn't worry too much if your child is a little behind on this list, or way beyond. As one teacher observes, "Some of my third graders are more like kindergartners, while others are doing fifth grade–level work."

If you're worried, however, or have any doubts about your child's readiness for third grade, you should talk to both his second grade teacher and his third grade teacher-to-be. Tutoring or some other form of extra help over the summer might make a significant difference.

Also, talk to the teachers if you're concerned that your child will be bored because he's working so far ahead of grade level. There may be a gifted program in your school that he can join, or the teachers might be able to suggest some enrichment activities for both home and school.

What to Expect in the Classroom

More work, harder work, and different ways of working. Instead of spending most of their time on mastering the basic skills, third graders are beginning to apply those skills to expand their learning.

The Big Switch

The biggest change in most (though not all) third grade classrooms is the shift to hardcover textbooks. You remember: the thick, heavy ones you had to cover with paper and you couldn't write in. There's a good chance your child will be issued four or five of them this year—one each for math, science, social studies, health, and English.

But it's not the books themselves that are significant. It's what they represent in terms of independent learning. From now on—even in classrooms that rely on soft-cover trade books and novel sets instead of traditional textbooks—you'll see a greater emphasis on *reading as a means of acquiring information.*

Your child will be doing more silent reading in the classroom and more independent research at home. She may have fewer worksheets and more assignments that require copying problems and other information from a textbook into a notebook. And she'll probably be expected to read more nonfiction materials in preparation for small-group or class discussions.

Your child may even start using textbooks to study for tests or to learn on her own new information about math, science, history, and social studies. "I was really surprised to find that in my daughter's third grade class, the teacher doesn't spend a lot of time at the blackboard giving lessons in math," says Peggy Schmidt, a mother of two. "Instead, each child moves through the math textbook at his or her own pace and goes to the teacher for mini-lessons and questions."

Give the Process Time

Making the transition from learning to read to reading to learn is easier for some children than others. Those who find it most difficult tend to be the ones who are struggling with reading to begin with. But even strong readers may feel intimidated at first, so it's important to be patient and supportive while this shift in learning takes place.

Most third grade teachers won't go cold turkey, anyway. They'll balance out the independent reading assignments with hands-on activities and real-life learning experiences.

The Importance of Tests

Prepare, too, for a greater emphasis on tests. In many schools, this is the year when graded pencil-and-paper tests become both prevalent and relevant. There are more tests, and more kinds of tests are given (not only timed tests but multiple choice, fill-in-the-blank, problem-solving, and oral tests, for example). And the grades your child gets on these tests may play a leading role on her report card.

This is also the year when many schools begin giving standardized tests, to see how their students compare with others locally, nationally, and statewide. (Some schools give standardized tests sooner, and some later, however. Check with your child's teacher or principal to find out your school's policy and schedule.)

Teachers say that it's not the tests themselves that are important in third grade, it's the process. Children need to learn how to study for tests and take them without getting too nervous, so they can succeed in their upcoming school years. (For more on testing, see "Measuring Progress," page 151.)

The Push for Independence

You'll probably notice other changes in the classroom this year. But the biggest one may be the teacher's expectation of independence—in everything from following classroom routines to budgeting time for homework and research projects. In class, the goal is to get children to the point where they can work on an assignment, either alone or in a small group, and if they finish their work early, they can think of something else to do—such as log on to the computer, pick up a book, or start another assignment.

Your child may complain that the teacher is "mean" or "strict" this year. But it's important to understand that third grade teachers are trying to prepare their students for the greater demands of the intermediate school years. Students who can work on their own and be responsible for both their successes and their failures will have an easier time when fourth and fifth grade roll around.

The Most Important Subject This Year

Aside from independence, it's literacy. That includes reading, writing, speaking, and listening. But, once again, reading is king.

Because of the switch to book-based learning, it's important for all children to be reading at or above grade level by now. If a child can't read at grade level, he's bound to have trouble in every single subject. By third grade, reading is required for everything from studying a textbook to following the directions on assignments and tests.

Here's a look at what to expect.

Reading

Teachers continue to use a variety of strategies to build reading skills. In some schools, children are divided into groups, based on reading levels, and taught specific skills by either their classroom teacher or another "reading" teacher. In other settings, children work in small reading groups within the classroom, but the groups change frequently and are not necessarily based on reading levels. Instead, they focus on a particular type or piece of literature, or on a science or social studies theme that the class is studying. Another approach is to pass out a text and workbooks in a reading series and allow each child to progress through the workbooks at his or her own pace.

In most third grades, there is also a regular time to visit the school library and take out books. There's a classroom library with fiction and nonfiction selections at a variety of reading levels. And children are expected to do lots of independent reading during the school day. Frequent book reports (about one a month) are assigned, and many teachers require students to do special reading-related projects, such as creating a poster to advertise their favorite book or dressing up as a character from a book and telling the class about an adventure that character had.

Usually, there is some exploration of different types of literature, from fables, legends, and myths to poetry, plays, fiction, and nonfiction. Students are regularly encouraged to read aloud, and reading is integrated into all other coursework, including math and science.

The emphasis throughout is on building vocabulary, knowledge, and comprehension—as well as a love of reading and a strong desire to read and learn.

Continue to Push

Any lag in reading skills should be seriously addressed. If your child was struggling earlier, he'll probably continue to get some kind of extra help at school, either from the teacher or from a tutor or reading specialist. You should also be working with him at home. If your child is not getting help and needs it, it's up to you to demand it. There is still time to strengthen his skills before the avalanche of work in fourth grade.

If your child is already a strong reader, you should keep encouraging him to read, so he can hone his vocabulary and comprehension skills. You should also keep reading to him.

Many parents assume that once a child can read on his own he doesn't need to be read to anymore. But according to teachers, that's absolutely not true. Reading aloud to your child will:

- enable him to enjoy books that are above his reading level, but not his interest level
- broaden his understanding of word usage and vocabulary
- expand his base of knowledge
- sharpen his listening and concentration skills
- give the two of you a good excuse to spend some one-on-one time together every day.

Most of all, it shows your child that you think reading is really important.

Writing

Expect, again, more independent work. In some classrooms, students spend as much as thirty to forty minutes a day developing their writing voice. In others, writing is required in some way in nearly every subject studied. While some children love this, others are beginning by now to think of writing as torture.

"My daughter really got into writing in third grade," says Peggy Schmidt. "She even wrote a story on her own and submitted it for a newspaper contest, which she won. But not everyone in her class feels as she does about writing. It seems like in third grade, there's a bigger chasm between the kids who are 'wired' to be writers and those who aren't."

Building Skills and Confidence

Most third grade teachers work hard to win the reluctant writers over, mainly by making writing assignments as interesting as possible. That includes encouraging children to try out different styles of writing, such as poetry, skits, news articles, stories, books, journal writing, notes to pen pals, and letters requesting information. It also involves getting them started with specific assignments, such as: write a new ending to your favorite book; keep a journal of your observations for this science experiment; or write a letter to your pen pal in Japan.

"Once you spark a child's interest and confidence, it's amazing what they can write," says Cyndy Novotny, of Woods Learning Center, in Casper, Wyoming. "I had one boy who was convinced he couldn't write and would struggle every day with the writing assignments. Then, one day, I discovered he was an expert on Disney World. So I asked him to write about that, and before I knew it he was producing page after page of copy."

Another strategy is to provide outlines and questions, to guide the students through each step of the writing assignment. "My daughter has to do at least one three-page book report a month," notes parent Ronnie Hochberg. "But she has a specific outline to follow, so it's not as intimidating as it might be." Included in the outline are questions like: Who is the main character? What is the crisis? What is the solution? and Describe one thing you liked/didn't like about this book.

Working the Process

There's much more emphasis on grammar, punctuation, and spelling in third grade. And children spend a good deal of time learning about the different parts of a sentence (what a subject, predicate, and adverb are, for instance). They also study synonyms, antonyms, and homonyms, so they can begin to refine their word-selection skills.

But there's usually plenty of time to perfect copy. As in second grade, writing is presented as a multi-stage process, and many assignments involve:

- *a pre-writing phase,* in which the children brainstorm and/or outline their ideas
- *a rough draft,* in which spelling and punctuation play second fiddle to ideas and organization
- *a revise,* based on input from the teacher and/or a writing partner, a small group of peer critics, or the entire class
- *an edit,* involving corrections by the teacher and/or a writing partner
- *a "published"* copy, or final draft.

The overall goal is to build each child's confidence, enjoyment of, and skill in putting thoughts into words on paper.

Encouraging Research

Longer-term writing projects and class presentations are

also part of the third grade landscape because teachers are now introducing note-taking and research skills.

The first step is learning how to copy information—from a book, a poster, the blackboard, an overhead projector, or even a computer screen, into a notebook or onto an index card or a sheet of loose-leaf paper. It takes a long time and a lot of practice for most children to get used to this, so teachers move slowly. For instance, the teacher might start the year by writing homework assignments on the board and reading them aloud as the children copy them onto assignment pads. By the middle of the year, she'll write them on the board and remind the children to copy them. By the end of the year, she might just write them down.

When it comes to research, there's usually some kind of instruction on using the library and various reference sources, such as atlases, dictionaries, encyclopedias, and card catalogs (computerized or tangible). Children also learn how to use a book's table of contents and index to locate specific information. Again, there's a lot of hand-holding at first, and assignments tend to be very specific, such as: "Read three sources with information about dinosaurs and write down five facts you've learned using your own words." By the end of the year, however, many children can take a topic and run with it.

Switching to Cursive

In many schools, third grade is when children start making the switch from printed to cursive writing. Even in the age of computers, this is still an important skill because it helps children take notes and write out assignments more quickly and efficiently. Someday, when every child in every classroom has access to a computer, this form of writing may die out. But based on today's rate of integrating technology into schools, that's probably a long way off.

In the beginning of the year, the children mainly learn how to form the cursive letters and connect them together. For some children this is relatively easy, but others may struggle with cursive until their fine motor skills and coordination become more developed. By the middle or end of the year, the teacher may require cursive writing for most assignments (though in some schools, this doesn't happen until fourth grade).

Children also need to learn to *read* in cursive, which is trickier than you'd think. There are so many different styles of handwriting that it's hard for an inexperienced reader to tell, sometimes, if a short loopy thing is an *a* or an *o* or even an *e*. This is yet another skill that takes practice. That's why teachers often switch midyear to using only cursive on the blackboard and on assignment sheets.

Speaking

Being able to explain ideas, ask questions, and communicate effectively is as important in independent learning as reading and writing. That's why many third grade teachers move public speaking up a notch and require more formal class—and sometimes school-wide—presentations. Children also build their speaking skills in third grade by working in teams, reading aloud in class, performing skits and plays, and sharing their experiences and treasures with classmates.

Many teachers admit they fiddle around with seating arrangements and team assignments, too, to make sure that children learn to work with partners who are not already their friends. And, of course, they make a special effort to call on the kids who don't raise their hands too often, to make sure those voices are heard.

These strategies may make your child uncomfortable and trigger some heartfelt complaints, but it's best to support the teacher. Eventually, the experiences will add to your child's ability to get along and communicate with different kinds of people, in different situations.

Other Important Subjects

Math and other subjects are also important in third grade. To get specifics on the curriculum at your child's school, you'll have to talk to his teacher or principal. But here's an overview of what goes on in many third grade classrooms.

Math

Third grade is a big year for math because children finally begin to move beyond addition and subtraction into single-digit multiplication and division. The beginning of the year, however, is usually devoted to reviewing and strengthening basic math facts. Children should be comfortable doing three-digit addition and subtraction before moving into multiplication.

If your child is struggling with the basic facts, you should talk to the teacher about what both of you can do to get him where he needs to be. Some schools have math specialists and basic skills teachers who can provide additional help.

Once your child's class starts getting serious about multiplication, you may see a greater emphasis on memorizing. This is partly because memorizing basic facts makes doing the more complicated math later on easier. But it's also because teachers are now keeping one eye on what the standardized tests require, and they know that on those, memorization helps.

Some children start getting scared of math at this point, because they find memorizing either difficult or boring. So most third grade teachers still do a lot to make math relevant and fun. They might use puzzles, songs, or games to teach multiplication facts, for instance, or work multiplication experiences into real-life problem solving.

More Advanced Math

Other typical third grade math goals include learning how to:

- recognize and write numbers up to 100,000
- round off numbers
- make reasonable estimations
- collect and graph data
- read and interpret different types of graphs
- measure length, area, volume, weight, and time using traditional and nontraditional units
- make change
- recognize and predict patterns
- identify and work with fractions.

In addition to using textbooks, many third grade teachers still use manipulatives—such as pattern blocks, base-ten blocks, fraction pieces, and money—to solidify math concepts. And most are still on the lookout for relevant, hands-on activities.

For instance, Karen Geiger, of Amy Beverland Elementary School, in Indianapolis, Indiana, has her class set up its own mini-society. At the beginning of the year, the children draw up a list of jobs, ranging from class sheriff to judge, librarian, accountant, banker, rest room monitor, and blackboard eraser. Then, each child interviews for the job he wants; once he gets it, he's responsible for that job for the entire year. But he also gets paid for it: $50 a week in "Geiger" dollars.

Some of the money must be used to pay "taxes," says Geiger, but the rest can be spent either in the classroom "store" (which sells everything from pencils and erasers to inexpensive picture frames and mugs that say "I love Mom" on them), or during the end-of-the-year carnival. "The students can also spend their money at our 'restaurants,'" says Geiger. In this math-related project, a team of children will come up with an idea for a restaurant, decide what they need to run it, determine a budget, and apply for a loan to buy the necessary materials. Then they'll advertise the restaurant and actually run it one day in the classroom.

"The children learn an amazing amount of math when they have to decide how to earn, budget, and spend their own 'money,'" says Geiger.

Science

There may be a greater focus on science this year, especially if your child has a textbook for this subject or her school has a special science teacher who rotates among classrooms. In fact, you may be amazed by what your third grader is learning—and doing.

"When I was growing up, science wasn't taught as an official classroom subject until I was in high school," recalls Peggy Schmidt. "In my daughter's school, they have a separate science teacher in third grade, and they do amazing things. Once, for example, the teacher brought in chicken parts and the children dissected them. Another time, they built their own musical instruments and she recorded their sounds."

Not every school is lucky enough to have a separate science specialist. But even in settings where science is taught only periodically by the classroom teacher, there's a greater emphasis on hands-on learning. Children don't just read about how a barometer works or watch the teacher demonstrate one, for instance; they make their own barometers, predict how they'll work, and observe them over a period of days or weeks. If they're studying electricity, they might get a chance to build their own homemade flashlight. Or, if they're studying life cycles, they might raise butterflies—from the tiny egg phase to the final, glorious unfolding of wings.

While carrying out their experiments, children learn to collect, classify, and record data, and compare and analyze results. "Even when a classroom experiment doesn't exactly work, the children learn from it," notes Karen Gunther. "It teaches them what real scientists know: that you often have to test a hypothesis over and over before you can draw a conclusion or verify results."

Topics vary from classroom to classroom, but among the more popular in third grade are: water cycles and the formation of clouds; animal and human bodies, and how they compare; rocks and minerals; the solar system; space exploration; and the various properties of matter.

Social Studies

Again, the addition of a textbook may make this a more-serious subject. But even if trade books are the norm in your child's classroom, you can expect more independent reading on social studies topics (including history, geography, civics, and, in some schools, character building and values). Also, there will probably be more emphasis on learning facts—and on taking tests.

That's not to say the subject will be totally dry. Many teachers back up the texts the children are reading with challenging experiences. For example, when her class was learning about the Pilgrims sailing on the *Mayflower*, Sharon Smith had her students overturn their tables, pile on with all their chairs and belongings, and think about how they'd feel if they had to travel across an ocean crowded in like that. In Edward Silver's classroom, during a unit on economics, each child had to design, produce, advertise, and sell a real product (such as paper airplanes).

Among the topics your child may be studying in third grade are: Native Americans; Pilgrims and early settlers; different regions of the United States and how they compare; inventors and inventions; basic economics; states and capitals; and maps and globes.

Computer

This may or may not be a separate course in your child's school. Some third grades have a cluster of computers in a corner of the classroom; others have access to a school computer lab where students go for special instruction once a week. But the bottom line is that most schools do not have the equipment (or teacher training) to make technology a major presence in the classroom.

Still, most third grade teachers make an effort to

ensure that all of their students have the chance to become familiar with computers, learn generally how they work, and use them independently for word processing and educational games.

Health

This subject might not be in your own third grade memory bank, but it's a major one in many third grade classrooms today. My son, Gus, even had a textbook for health in third grade. It covered everything from the importance of developing a strong self-concept and healthy eating and lifestyle habits to avoiding the unhealthful effects of drugs, tobacco, and alcohol.

Many third grade teachers say that health-related discussions are among the most lively—and most important—in their classrooms. They also say that the perfect time to get children thinking about healthy living and making positive choices is *before* peer pressure kicks in.

If your child's classroom teacher isn't teaching health, there's a good chance the subject will come up in physical education, which should still play an important role in your child's school experience.

Art and Music

Every school has its own approach to these subjects. You can probably expect more this year of what your child already experienced in first and second grade. Especially important are lots of opportunities to experiment, explore, and create. If your child's school is cutting down on art and music at this point, you should look for extracurricular ways to keep your child involved, even if he complains because he's not that great at drawing or he can't carry a tune. He can always try working with another medium, such as clay, or learn how to play an instrument. (In many schools, this is the year when the recorder is taught.) Remember, in third grade it's the process, not the product, that's important.

Homework—and How to Help

The easy years are behind you. From now on, you can count on your child getting lots of homework, and you can almost bet that at some point soon she'll start to complain about it. As Daniel Cunningham notes, "At first, my son really liked having homework, because it made him feel grown-up. But toward the end of the year, it became more of a battle. I think the work got harder, and he got tired of always having it."

What to Expect

Most third grade teachers give anywhere from thirty to forty-five minutes of homework a night, though it can take up to an hour. Fridays are often homework-free, unless there's a book report or special project due on Monday.

Since most homework is designed to back up whatever the teacher is teaching in class, it'll probably be fairly rote—and, for you, comfortably familiar. Your child may have spelling words to put into sentences and memorize, for instance, or a page of math problems to work out. He may be assigned a chapter to read in his social studies or health textbook, or be given a worksheet related to grammar or reading comprehension. He'll probably have some additional reading, and he may have a test to study for.

In some schools, children also receive homework

designed to reinforce specific character traits or values, such as kindness, responsibility, respect, and motivation. For example, to reinforce the concept of responsibility, the assignment might be: "Write down all of the chores you do this week and make a graph showing how much time you spend on each one."

The Parent's Role

Most third grade teachers want their students to take more responsibility for their own homework. "We really want the child—not the parent—to pack and unpack the book bag, write down homework assignments, and hand the work in now," notes Susan Jameson, of Boyertown Elementary School in Pennsylvania. To encourage this, teachers use different strategies that help their students remember what needs to be done and when. Some even hand out monthly planning calendars marked with the due dates of long-term projects, reports, and tests.

Your job is mainly to help your child find a time and a place to get the work done. There's no formula here: Pick a time that's convenient for your child and a place that's relatively private. Do what you can to make the homework location special, so your child will begin to think of it as his own little office.

When he's finished with his homework, look it over. If there are careless mistakes, or if it's especially messy, have him fix it. Third grade teachers expect homework to be relatively neat and error-free; some even grade it.

If your child doesn't understand an assignment, and you can't easily explain it, don't force the issue. Send it back to the teacher with a note explaining that your child needs more instruction.

Many third grade teachers also require the parent to sign the finished homework (mainly to verify that you've taken the time to be involved in your child's schoolwork).

Prepare for Trouble

If you're extremely lucky, that's all you'll have to do. But if you're just a normal, overworked parent with a normal eight-year-old kid, your involvement will likely go further. A quick poll of parents at my local playground revealed a host of homework-related problems. Their children (many of them very good students) frequently do things like:

- complain that the homework is "too hard" or "too boring"
- put it off until the last minute, and then rush through it, making unnecessary mistakes
- do such a sloppy job that you can't tell if the answers are correct
- cry if they can't get everything perfect
- forget to copy the assignments from the blackboard
- forget to bring home the necessary worksheets or textbooks from school
- say they finished everything when they actually haven't
- say they have no homework when they actually do
- do the homework and then forget to take it to school or hand it in
- suddenly remember they have a big test or project— the night before it's due.

Winning the Battle

When homework problems pop up, get your child involved in solving them. Sometimes homework resistance appears because the work itself is too difficult for a child. In that case, you may want to give more help with figuring out the instructions. If that doesn't work, talk to the teacher about modifications.

If your child seems able—but not willing—to do the homework, modify the homework routine. In some cases, a change in time or location can make a difference. Or, your child may benefit from taking a break from the homework every ten minutes or so. She may even need an external motivator, as in: "If you finish all your homework before supper, you can watch a video before bed."

The key is to make it clear that homework is not negotiable: It must be done. If all else fails, you may just have to let your child suffer the consequences of a lower grade for forgetting to do the homework or to pass it in. As one teacher notes, "It's better for your child to experience the negative consequences in third grade than to learn the hard way in fifth or sixth."

Measuring Progress

Letter grades and tests. Whether you love them or hate them, you've got to start living with them now. In most third grades, they're the main signposts of problems and success. How you react to them will determine in large part how your child feels about his performance and progress in school.

Grades

At first, grades may not mean too much to your child. But it usually doesn't take long for a third grader to begin comparing his grade to his classmates'—and drawing conclusions from there. In many classrooms, the "I got an A—what did you get?" routine begins early in the year. By the end, almost any child in the class can spout off a list of the kids who are doing the best—and the worst—in every subject.

Parents play the deciding role, however. Your child will start thinking of grades as his main measure of success if you're constantly asking questions like: "Who's the smartest in your class?"; "Did anyone else get a higher grade than you?"; or "What's this C all about? You can't get into a good college with grades like that!"

A better approach is to treat grades as what they're meant to be: a guide to what your child has learned and what he needs to work on. When you see an A, praise the effort that went into earning it, as in: "Congratulations. All that hard work you've been doing has really paid off." When you see a lower-than-expected grade, let your child know the world is not ending: "You tried your best, and I'm really proud of that. Maybe next time, I could show you a few tricks I learned to help me prepare for tests."

What Grades Don't Tell

Even if your child isn't getting all A's, it doesn't mean she's doing poorly. "To me, a good student isn't necessarily one who gets all A's and B's," notes Karen Gunther. "It's one who is trying hard and developing strong study habits. Parents need to appreciate the progress their child is making, not just focus on the grades."

It may help to remind yourself that most colleges do not look at third grade report cards when accepting students. What's most important right now is helping your child feel successful and learn the necessary skills, so that when grades really do begin to matter (in middle and high school), he'll be ready to do his best.

If your child is getting consistently low grades or shows a sudden drop in grades you should talk to his teacher. Other behaviors that should concern you include *frequent:*

- complaints about the difficulty or amount of work required
- episodes of stress-related illnesses, such as stomach-aches and headaches
- physical expressions of tension, such as nail-biting, hair-pulling, throat-clearing, or chewing on pencils, hair, or clothes
- battles over homework
- displays of anger, irritation, and frustration
- requests to play with younger children, or a lack of interest in play dates with classmates.

If these types of behaviors are common, talk to the teacher—no matter what your child's grades are.

Tests

When it comes to tests, focus on how your child *feels* about taking them, rather than on how high she scores. In third grade, tests exist not only to measure knowledge and progress, but to prepare children for what lies ahead.

Because of their inexperience, third graders are often easily thrown off during test situations. Too much noise in the classroom, for instance, or too little breakfast in the tummy can cause an A student to pull a C. So you shouldn't get too concerned over individual test grades. That will only make your child anxious—and more likely to make careless mistakes on the next test.

Teaching the Basics

To build confidence and self-esteem, most third grade teachers try to maximize their students' success on tests by giving lots of pretest hints and help. That may involve hanging up signs that give definitions of key words that'll appear on an upcoming test; sending home a study guide with sample questions; or giving the children a practice test that they can take together in teams.

Teachers also usually provide guidance on how to study. For example, before a big test, students might be instructed to follow these six steps:

1. Find a partner (a parent, older sibling, classmate, or friend).
2. Have that person ask you the questions on the study sheet (or make up questions based on information in the textbook).
3. Have your partner circle the questions you get wrong.
4. Go back to your textbook to find the correct answers to the questions you missed.
5. Write down the correct answers, to help yourself remember them.
6. Repeat the process, until you get every question right.

Test-Taking Hints

When it comes to *taking* tests, teachers stress three basics:

1. Read the directions carefully before you pick up your pencil. If you don't understand something, ask the teacher right away, before you attempt any answers.
2. Skim the entire test to see what kinds of questions there are, so you can budget your time appropriately.
3. If you come to a question you can't answer (on a timed test), circle it and move ahead. If there's time at the end, go back and work on the problems you circled.

More Ways to Help

If the teacher isn't teaching these skills, you should do so at home. It will also help if you:

- minimize your interest in test scores and grades, so your child won't think that getting a good grade is more important than learning
- encourage your child to start studying days in advance, instead of trying to cram in knowledge the night before
- make yourself available to quiz your child before a test, and help him identify the weak links in his knowledge
- encourage him to write down key pieces of information, so he can review and remember them more easily

- make sure he gets a good night's sleep before the test and eats a nutritious breakfast before going to school
- review test results, to help your child see why he made certain mistakes, and what he could do differently the next time.

Standardized Tests

Different schools have different policies about standardized testing. But in many school systems, third grade is the year when group testing either begins or is taken more seriously. So be prepared: At some point in the year, your child's entire class may be given one or more standardized tests to measure:

- *achievement in basic skills,* such as reading, math, and social studies (examples include the California Achievement Test [CAT], the Metropolitan Achievement Test [MAT], the Iowa Tests of Basic Skills [ITBS], the Stanford Achievement Tests [SAT], and the Sequential Test of Education Progress [STEP])

- *overall intelligence,* including reasoning and memory skills (e.g., the Kuhlman-Anderson Test [KAT], and the Cognitive Abilities Test [COGAT]).

These tests are known as standardized tests because they involve specific rules that everyone who takes them must follow. This is so important, in fact, that most teachers give their students practice tests beforehand, so they'll feel comfortable with the testing procedures when the official test is given.

Standardized tests also use the same measurements to gauge each student's performance. The scores are designed to show where an individual child stands in comparison to other children of the same age, or in the same grade (either nationally, regionally, or locally). They aren't like classroom grades, however. A 50 percent on a classroom test might mean the child performed poorly, but on a standardized test it would mean that the child did an average job—or just as well as most third graders.

How Teachers Use Them

Though some schools use standardized test scores when making student placement decisions, most teachers say they use them mainly to make sure that their curriculum and teaching strategies are on target.

Parents should look at the scores, but not worry about them. They are not accurate predictors of future success. And there are many factors that can throw a child off on these tests. If a score is lower than expected, it's often because something happened at home the night before or the child didn't get a good night's sleep or she had a fight with her friend before school.

If a child scores higher than expected, the teacher might look at why her abilities are not being expressed in schoolwork. But most teachers say they don't get too many surprises. In third grade, the main value of these tests is in preparing children for the major exams they'll be taking further down the road.

If you have any questions about the type, frequency, or attitude of your child's school toward standardized testing, or what it eventually does with the test scores, talk to the teacher, school counselor, or principal.

Otherwise, the best thing you can do when the testing

begins is tell your child: "Relax. Do your best, and that will be fine."

What to Expect on the Social Scene

This is the year when boys and girls decide they don't want to be seen together in public. They may still be friends in one-on-one situations and work well together in teams at school. They may even spend a great deal of time whispering about who likes whom. But outside on the playground, they cluster in same-sex groups.

The girl groups tend to place high value on loyalty (though the loyalties shift all the time). Feelings can be easily hurt if one member spends "too much" time with another, or says something "mean." Boys still take more of a love-the-one-you're-with approach. They'll hang out with anyone who wants to play the same game.

Conflicts tend to be less common, but you still see eruptions—from kids picking on each other, calling each other names, tattling, blaming, excluding, and complaining about fairness. Eight- and nine-year-olds are much more capable of talking problems out, however, and listening to reason when disagreements occur. If you set a good example, they'll try to follow it.

Deeper Friendships

Not all children want—or need—a best friend at this point, so you shouldn't worry too much if your child doesn't have one. If he has a group of friends and seems to get along relatively well with most of them most of the time,

that's enough for now. (If he has *no* friends or is s
by his classmates, you should definitely be concer
talk to the teacher.)

When "best friends" are involved, you can expect your
child to be more choosy. "My daughter is much more sensitive about her friends' behaviors this year," notes one
mother. "For example, there's one girl she's been friends
with since she was four who tends to be fairly bossy. My
daughter used to just go along with the girl, but now
she's stepping back and questioning their relationship.
She doesn't want to give in as much. She's struggling
with wanting to branch out to other girls who seem more
compatible and not wanting to hurt her old friend's feelings."

Peer Pressure

Complications may also arise as a result of peer pressure. Its presence will probably be subtle this year, but
you'll definitely notice it, especially toward May and
June. For example, your child might:

- start begging to have a certain toy, piece of clothing,
  or special haircut—so his classmates will think he's
  cool
- come home from school in tears because she wasn't
  invited to a birthday party—and "everyone else" was
- start talking about who the "popular" kids are (big
  surprise: It's usually the prettiest girls and the most
  athletic boys)
- complain if you suggest he invite an "uncool" kid over
  for a play date—or make him accept that child's invitation

- walk a bit ahead of you—and shrug off your touch—
  when you're in the mall or on the street
- worry excessively about something "stupid" she said
  or wore in public.

This is only the beginning. And it's worse in some places than in others. "It seems like children are growing up much faster these days," notes Anne Arjani, a mother of two. "In my daughter's school, you can already see the herd mentality beginning to click. When the most popular girl in her class got a short haircut, for example, four other girls had theirs cut, too. There's also already a lot of pressure to listen to certain kinds of music, watch more grown-up television shows, and wear certain styles of clothing. Among the girls, there's less running around on the playground and more huddling in circles talking about boys. Some kids even have boyfriends! The children who don't have strong social skills right now are beginning to feel lost."

Be There

The best you can do, at this point, is keep reinforcing those conflict resolution skills and be there to listen when your child really needs you. "Every night, I sit with my daughter and help her process the politics of the day," says Anne Arjani. "We talk about everything from being bullied to making friends to playing with boys. I cherish these moments, though, because I know in a few years she's only going to want to talk about these things with her friends."

"I feel like my son is trying a lot of ideas out on me these days," says another mother. "He won't say anything direct, like, 'I really like this girl.' Instead, he'll say 'So-and-so in my class is in love with this girl, and they've already kissed.' Then he waits to see how I react."

Again, it's important to find the time to talk to your child and listen to what he has to say. As one teacher notes, "Third graders are still innocent and bonded to their parents, but that's not going to last much longer. Soon they'll be turning to their peers for advice."

The After-School Schedule

Your biggest concern when making after-school plans should be homework. If your child is loaded down with it, or if he views it as another burden in an already draining academic day, you'll want to go easy on the extracurricular schedule. As Daniel Cunningham notes, "I ended up cutting out most of my son's weekday activities in third grade because all he really wanted to do in the afternoons was either retreat to his own room for some solitary play or run around in the park with his buddies."

"My daughter was the one to tell me to cut back," says Pam Allen. "She said she felt overbooked and wanted to spend more time playing at home."

The nice part about third graders playing at home (or in a relatively unstructured after-school care situation) is that they usually know exactly what they want to do, and they can often amuse themselves. Kids this age love to play games, they love to admire and add to their collections of various "things," and some of them even love to have free time to write or read.

Striking a Balance

In addition to playing alone, third graders love spending time with their friends. And they're often eager to move their bodies around after being cooped up in a classroom. So anything that involves socializing and movement is generally appealing, whether it's running around and riding bikes in the neighborhood or joining a class in dance, karate, skating, swimming, or gymnastics after school. If your child has participated in these activities before, you may notice exciting strides this year, thanks to her greater strength and coordination.

The same goes for organized team sports. Third graders are better at playing baseball, soccer, basketball, and other sports, and they're better at remembering the rules. In fact, kids this age tend to learn the rules of a game quickly—and then argue about the finer points vehemently. But they aren't quite as good at actually following the rules, so you can't expect too much. It's still too soon to push your child into a rigid or highly competitive league.

Activities that involve finer motor skills—such as sewing, weaving, painting, woodworking, or learning to play an instrument—are also good choices now, because children can do more with them.

There is no set formula for what your child should do, however. The best advice is: Follow his interests as much as possible, while keeping a close eye on energy and stress levels. And let him explore different kinds of activities, instead of trying to specialize in one. If there's something he develops a passion for, he can always return to it later, after he's discovered for himself what else he's good at and likes to do.

Plan in Family Time

When it comes to play dates, you mainly have to be careful that you don't schedule in too many. As Peggy Schmidt notes, "Socializing after school hits a new frenzy in third grade. There are a lot more play dates scheduled during the week, and there are birthday parties and sleepovers on the weekends. My daughter could easily go a whole weekend without ever sleeping in her own bed. I find that every now and then I just have to say, 'No. No more play dates. You're spending time with *me* today!'"

Teachers wish many parents would do that more often. As one principal notes, "Third graders may not look as cuddly and vulnerable as first and second graders, but deep down they're just little kids. They still need—and want—to spend time with their parents." But that impulse won't last forever.

*F*ourth grade is the bridge that connects early childhood to preadolescence. It's when the skills that were learned in the primary grades (such as reading, writing, and math) get put to work as tools for learning. It's when children begin to see a greater depth to themselves and notice more of the world around them. And, most of all, it's a time when individuality and independence begin to flourish.

As Joan Lenowitz, a mother of two, notes, "In third grade, my daughter could do a lot on her own, but she was tentative. She'd often be wondering 'Should I be doing this?' or 'Is this the right way?' In fourth grade, she stopped wondering and just started doing."

STAYING INVOLVED

In many ways, this is a wonderful age. Fourth graders aren't so grown-up that they can't enjoy an adult's company. But they're not so young that they have to depend on you for everything. They can amuse themselves now, they can take care of many of their own needs, and they're getting better at listening and responding to reason.

In addition, most nine-year-olds are ready for the challenges of this school year and are eager to be more grown-up. In fact, you may start thinking it's a good time to pull back and be less involved in school. Or you may start assuming that the teacher is taking care of everything.

But according to teachers, that just isn't true. As Judy Sheldon, of Booker T. Washington Elementary School, in Dover, Delaware, notes, "No teacher can give a room full of nine-year-olds all of the academic, emotional, and moral support they need.

"The most successful students in my classroom are still the ones whose parents stay involved with what's happening at school," adds Sheldon. They ask about homework, they look over the textbooks, and they call the teacher when there are questions or problems. They also stay on top of who their child's friends are and what their child is reading or watching on TV. And they take the time to talk to their children and listen to what their children have to say.

"It definitely takes more effort to stay involved," adds Sally Vesty, a mother of three. "By fourth grade, you're not going into your child's classroom as much, and you're not hanging out on the playground talking with other parents," she explains. "So you really have to work at staying in touch with school."

THE PAYOFF

Is it worth the effort? Absolutely. Adolescence comes earlier these days, and it brings far more conflicts and choices than most of us could ever have imagined. At younger and younger ages, our children are being pressured to smoke cigarettes and experiment with drugs and alcohol. They're living in a world where students carry guns to school to shoot other students, and sexual activity can lead to not only pregnancy, but to disease and death.

These probably won't be big issues in fourth grade. But it's important to realize you have only a few more years left to enjoy your child's childhood and help him build the confidence and inner strength he'll need to survive—and thrive—in middle school and beyond.

What Fourth Graders Are Like

They're like third graders—with attitude. You still see a lot of energy and enthusiasm in fourth grade, and a real thirst for knowledge. But you also see more questioning of authority.

"The biggest change from third to fourth grade was in my son's attitude," says Jane Murray, a mother of four. "If I ask him to do something now, he won't just get up and do it like he used to. He'll say, 'After I finish this' or 'I don't think I should have to' or 'Maybe I'll do it later.' It's as though he's suddenly decided that adults aren't the only ones who get to make the rules."

Other parents say their fourth graders have turned into little know-it-alls. "If I say something that's wrong, my son can't wait to correct me," notes one father. "And if I express an opinion on something, he'll jump right in with his own views on the subject. He even tries to tell me how to fix things—like the car or the oven—that he couldn't possibly know how to fix!"

Fourth graders are also famous for complaining ("It's not fair—I'm *always* the one who has to clear the table!") and justifying bad behavior ("It's not my fault I left my homework at home. You made me take a bath last night, so I couldn't put it in my backpack").

"Kids this age like to be right, and they like to make their own rules," says Sally Vesty. "They think that they know what's best now, and they want *adults* to go along with *them*."

Learning to Let Go

Fourth grade defiance is not a sign that your child has been poorly raised or is heading for trouble. It's mainly a way for her to announce "I'm growing up now, so give me more space."

The best response is remaining calm. "Whenever I hear my daughter say 'I don't have to' or 'You can't make me,' I try not to react too strongly," notes Joan Lenowitz. "I view it as her way of finding out how serious I am, and what her boundaries are. Instead of getting upset, I spell out the consequences of her not cooperating, and let her decide what to do."

It'll also help if you give your child more autonomy. Fourth graders see themselves as more grown-up, and they want to be treated with the respect they believe they deserve. In particular, they want the freedom to voice their opinions (on every possible subject), and some ongoing evidence that they're being heard.

So whenever you feel it's safe and appropriate, step back and let your fourth grader negotiate a better deal or take charge of a situation that directly affects her (such as deciding when to do homework, what to buy for school, or what to pack for lunch). Listen to her arguments about why she should or shouldn't have to do something before you make your final decision.

Staying in Charge

You don't always have to say yes to your child's requests. (In fact, you shouldn't if you think your child is asking for something that's inappropriate or unsafe.) And there may be times when your child is so persistent that the only way you can end a conversation is to firmly state, "Because I said so!" But, in general, try to start viewing your child as a big kid, not a little one. As one parent notes, "You don't have much choice, anyway. By fourth grade, you can't control your child's life the way you could in preschool. You're losing the control—and your child wants it." So you might as well hand it over in small, safe doses.

That includes letting your child learn some lessons the hard way. For example, if he doesn't do his homework on time or flunks a test because he forgot to study don't make excuses to the teacher: Let him suffer the consequences of a lower grade. If he insists on staying up until midnight reading, let him try it once—and see how he feels the next day.

Fourth graders are beginning to see cause-and-effect relationships more clearly and can learn a lot from real-life experiences. When a child makes a bad choice and fails, for instance, she learns about making better choices and builds her ability to cope with disappointment. These skills will help her later on, when she's older and the stakes are higher.

Defiance at School

Parents aren't the only targets of fourth grade defiance. Teachers must face it, too. They no longer get supreme status just because they're the teacher. They have to win their students over. And even then, it can be difficult to get some fourth graders to buckle down and do their schoolwork.

Different teachers have different ways of responding to defiance. But what seems to work best is a clear-cut system of discipline. For instance, in Judy Sheldon's classroom, each child has an index card that gets "punched out" (with a hole puncher) whenever there's an infraction of classroom rules or a child refuses to cooperate. One hole in the card is a warning, two holes means the child has to write in his behavior journal, three holes means a loss of recess or some other privilege, and four holes (in one day) means an automatic phone call to the parents.

"Once the students know exactly what will happen if they don't behave, and they see you're consistent, there's usually less defiance," notes Sheldon. And there's often more enthusiasm and loyalty. (Fourth graders still *want* to please their teacher and their parents—it's just not their first priority anymore.)

Deference to Peers

When it comes to pleasing peers, there's a whole different story. Most children in this grade will do almost anything to win the support and admiration of their classmates. As one father notes, "At home, my daughter acts very self-assured and confident and is almost always certain that she's right. When she's with a group of peers, however, she's a different person. She's shy and cautious, and very sensitive to peer pressure."

This kind of duality shouldn't alarm you. This is the age of name-calling and note-passing. It's when children start homing in on how they compare to their classmates and begin to care deeply about what their peers will think. There's a greater awareness of who's popular and who's not and a stronger tendency to tease and exclude those who are "different."

Your child may seem more competitive or more self-conscious this year, and "fitting in" may become a major goal.

Other Leading Traits

What else can you expect from your child this year?

- *More help around the house.* Fourth graders can get themselves ready for school, make their own lunches, clean their own rooms, and remember to do their homework. They can also do a respectable job with chores such as vacuuming, dusting, setting the table, cleaning up after supper, helping with the grocery list, helping with the laundry, or even occasionally cooking.

  This is a good time to hand over more responsibility for household chores, because learning to be responsible at home fortifies independent learning at school. And even though your child might complain about doing chores, they can help him feel more competent and self-reliant.

  Keep in mind, however, that fourth graders do best when given a specific, doable task—and minimal supervision. For instance, don't say "It's your job to clean the kitchen" and then second-guess everything your child does ("No, put the plates away first" or "Use the broom this way"). Try: "I'd like you to clear the table, rinse the plates, and put them in the dishwasher." Then leave the room until your child is finished. When he's done his job well (don't expect perfection), say so.

- *More sensitivity.* Fourth graders are very aware of who can do what in school. And they're much more concerned about what other kids think. So instead of getting angry because something wasn't fair ("Tyler took two cookies and I only got one!"), they're more likely to complain because of hurt feelings and bruised pride ("Sam is telling everyone I'm a cheater!" or "Mary and Kathy say I'm spoiled and won't play with me"). Fourth graders also get easily embarrassed when they can't do something or when they make a mistake and other kids laugh.

  But they're especially sensitive about schoolwork. Up until now, for instance, children with learning difficulties are often hardly aware that they're any different from their peers. But in fourth grade, they become acutely aware and can feel devastated when they lag behind.

  It's important to keep encouraging your child to take risks and recognize her own success at this stage. Also, be generous with praise—especially when your child asks for it (as in: "Did you see that home run I hit?" or "Don't you think I did a great job on my project?"). Positive feedback that's specific and realistic can have a powerful effect on confidence and self-esteem.

- *More socializing.* Fourth grade teachers describe their students as gregarious, ebullient, and extremely sociable. They're constantly buzzing, and they seem to have a million things to talk about. In fact, at times it takes a lot of effort to get them to focus on schoolwork.

  In the primary grades, if a teacher snaps at the students to quiet down, they usually shape up right away. But with fourth graders, teachers say, you can stand on your head and ask them twenty times to pull out their books—and they'll still keep talking about who they're going to sit with at lunch.

  Plus, they never seem to get sick of each other. As one teacher notes, "Even when it comes to going to the bathroom, they want to take a friend."

  While the constant talking and socializing can drive an adult crazy, the desire to interact with peers is a definite advantage when it comes to working in groups in the classroom. That's why many fourth grade teachers do all they can to promote cooperative learning. As Helene Blackman, a teacher at Eagle Elementary School, in West Bloomfield, Michigan, notes, "Even a simple assignment becomes more motivating when it can be done with a friend."

- *More persistence.* Like their younger peers, fourth graders want to be good at things, and they love to win. But now they have the tools and the attention span to really develop their interests and skills. They're also more goal-oriented and more willing to do something over and over again, until they get it right.

  "My son is beginning to set goals for himself and work toward them on his own," says Judy Bloom, a mother of two. "For instance, he wanted to improve his cursive handwriting this year, so he took it upon himself to practice at home, until he got better."

This kind of dedication can lead to wonderful accomplishments and generate lots of pride. But if your child's persistence turns into perfectionism, you may see the reverse. Perfectionists tend to set rigid and unreasonably high goals for themselves, and they interpret small failures as sweeping evidence of their lack of competence or self-worth.

If you notice that your child is constantly working at something, but is never happy with her performance, or if she puts off doing required schoolwork because she's afraid she won't do it perfectly, talk to her teacher. She may need help setting more reasonable goals and learning to live with less-than-perfect results.

- *More growth.* Some children look quite young in fourth grade, but an increasing number are beginning to shoot up and fill out. There may even be some girls in the class who are beginning to need a bra or to menstruate.

  If your child is on a faster track with development, you should already be talking about the physical and emotional changes that accompany puberty. If your child starts noticing she's gaining weight and becomes worried, reassure her that her body is simply preparing itself for the growth spurts ahead; if she seems preoccupied about her appearance, have her talk to a pediatrician.

  A fourth grader should *not* be dieting, exercising excessively, or lifting weights. Nor should a child be so worried about being attractive and thin, or strong and muscular, that he or she can't enjoy life. Unfortunately, in our weight-conscious culture, many nine-year-olds are already anxious about the size and shape of their bodies. So you should try to be careful about making comments on how your child looks. Offhand remarks and teasing ("Looks like you're getting a little chubby there" or "Hey, skinny Minnie!") can make a deeper impression than you intended.

Don't buy into your child's fears about appearance and weight, either (by suggesting a diet program or a workout routine). While nine is still too young for body sculpting, it is not too soon for an eating disorder or low self-esteem to develop. Instead, encourage your child to stay active, eat healthy foods, and appreciate the changes her body is going through. It will help shore up her confidence and self-concept when the pressure to look perfect intensifies later on.

The Rate of Change

How quickly your fourth grader experiences any of these changes will depend on a variety of factors, such as where he lives, who his friends are, who his teacher is, what he's allowed to watch on television, whether or not he has older siblings, and how rapidly his body is developing. So keeping up with the kid next door should not be a goal.

Nor should you feel pressured to give in to requests that you think are unreasonable just because your child insists that "Everyone else in my class gets to do it!" or "So-and-so's parents say it's okay." Those claims tend to be overblown, anyway. And there's no reason to rush your child to grow up.

Fourth graders still need parents to set reasonable—and firm—limits on everything from how late they stay up to how much time they spend with friends and what they watch on TV. They also need lots of support and encouragement in discovering what they're good at and what they like to do. And they need to hear over and over again that disappointments, failures, and mistakes are simply opportunities for learning (rather than predictions of ability or measures of self-worth).

The most important thing, however, is to enjoy your fourth grader—while he still enjoys you. As teacher Frances Sergi, of Kew-Forest, notes, "Children this age have a curiosity that's really beautiful. They're noticing everything now, and they want to learn more and more. But they're still fairly innocent and accepting. They don't carry the baggage of hatred and bigotry yet. And though they do get angry, they forgive and forget quickly."

Appreciate these qualities while they last.

What Fourth Graders Should Know

By now your child should be a fairly accomplished learner, with a strong foundation of basic skills. Fourth grade teachers like to see children enter their classrooms with the ability to:

- read chapter books—for research and recreation
- pick out books at the library and read on their own for fun
- use a dictionary to find out how a word is spelled, what it means, or how it's pronounced
- find information in a book by looking at its table of contents, glossary, or index

- pay attention during class lessons and follow verbal instructions with minimal or no help
- read and follow written instructions independently
- write a one-page story or book report that includes a distinct beginning, a middle, and an end
- ask questions, and be able to use basic reference skills to find answers
- answer written and verbal questions in complete sentences ("The boy was angry because his dog chased a cat down the street" instead of "because the dog was running")
- understand and perform basic computations (using addition, subtraction, multiplication, and division)
- recognize and write numbers up to 100,000
- round off numbers, and be able to estimate, measure, collect and graph data, and work with simple fractions
- relate number problems to real-life situations (4 x 2 could mean four sets of two books), and solve them
- use cursive writing for most assignments
- turn on and use a computer for word processing, educational games, or simple research
- work cooperatively in a group instead of shrinking back or taking over.

A Tougher Year

If these expectations seem high it's because the work gets more intense in fourth grade. There's a stronger push toward independent reading and research. And there is far more emphasis on analyzing and comparing. In addition to examining the "who" and "what" questions ("Who were the Pilgrims?" and "What happens when you plant a seed?"), for instance, fourth graders spend a lot of time exploring the "whys" and "hows" ("Why did the Pilgrims leave England?"; "Why do immigrants come to America today?"; and "How can you make a seed grow better?").

While some fourth graders are more than ready for all this, others need help making the transition. "Moving from third to fourth grade is a big step for many children," notes teacher Cathy Pihl, of Kate Bond Elementary School, in Memphis, Tennessee. "Even those who are used to getting all A's and B's may start bringing home C's for a while." Or, for the first time, you may be hearing comments like "It's too hard" or "I can't do it" or "I stink at math."

Finding Support

Extra support and encouragement will help most children get used to the academic challenges. But if you're worried that your child won't be able to keep up or that he'll need more hands-on help, talk to the teacher. She, too, may be concerned if your child:

- seems socially or emotionally immature compared to his peers, especially if he's the youngest in his class
- is unable to follow instructions and work independently
- prefers playing with younger children
- is having trouble keeping up with third grade work or remembering things he previously learned
- is showing signs of stress, such as frequent headaches and stomachaches, or often makes excuses not to go to school.

What to Expect in the Classroom

- More formality. Fourth grade marks the begin ... ... the intermediate years, when the pace of learning picks up. Children are now being groomed for the greater demands of middle school and junior high, so many (though not all) schools switch to a more traditional approach. For example, you may notice:

- *A more structured school day.* It's more likely than ever that your child's schedule will be separated into distinct thirty- to forty-minute periods, and that each period will be assigned a specific subject, such as social studies, math, reading, or science. These subjects should not be taught strictly as stand-alones, however. Your child should still be learning to make connections between the various subjects he's studying, and the teacher should still be using reading, writing, and math to enhance learning in social studies, science, and other areas.

   One of the major goals in fourth grade is to teach students to look at *whatever* they're learning and ask: "How does this relate to other things I've learned or other experiences I've had?" and "What does this teach me about myself and my world?"

- *More emphasis on textbooks.* If your child didn't have them in third grade, he'll surely have them in fourth. But don't expect the teacher to follow any prepackaged learning materials exactly. (In fact, *hope* that she doesn't. Textbooks haven't gotten much more interesting since we parents were kids. And our media-saturated children are bound to consider them even more bland and boring than we did.)

Most teachers will use the textbooks (or other standardized learning materials) more as curriculum guides than as teaching tools. Often, they'll introduce a subject with an interesting, hands-on activity in the classroom, and then assign from the text for homework. Though fourth graders are getting better at book learning, they still need firsthand experiences.

- *More involvement with specialist teachers.* While some fourth graders spend their day in a self-contained classroom with one teacher, others begin to move around the school more. For example, they may spend a few hours each day with a teacher who specializes in language arts and social studies and then move to another classroom and a different teacher for science and math. They may also move around for instruction in a foreign language or computer use and have separate teachers for art, music, and gym.

Still Expect Diversity

Not all classrooms or daily schedules will look the same, however. So don't get too worried if your child experiences some or none of the above. Her teacher may have a different strategy that'll be just as effective in meeting the school's fourth grade curriculum goals. If you have any questions about the classroom, the daily schedule, the learning materials, or the curriculum, talk to your child's teacher or the school principal.

The Most Important Subject This Year

Getting organized. Now that they have the basic skills in place, children are expected to use those skills to explore academic subjects in greater depth. That usually involves more independent reading and research and more long-term papers and projects. To complete these tasks without pulling out their hair (and yours), children need to learn to manage both time and information. By middle school and junior high, these organizational skills will be essential.

Two of your child's most important appendages this year will be a loose-leaf notebook, with colorful dividers for different subjects, and a calendar. In-class assignments and homework may be given on a weekly basis now, instead of day-by-day, and longer-term projects may be given each month. The notebook and calendar will help both of you keep track of what needs to be handed in, and when.

In class, the teacher may emphasize the various steps involved in completing different learning tasks. In writing, for instance, the first draft/revise/edit/final draft progression may be stressed, and children may spend more time analyzing the various components of quality work (as in, "What makes this an A paper?"). In addition, the teacher and students may work together on developing rubrics, to ensure that the most important bases are covered in an assignment. And step-by-step guidelines may be given for studying, taking notes, taking tests, and writing papers.

Helping at Home

Some children are born to organize, and for them, fourth grade may be a cinch. But most children need to be taught how to approach assignments and tasks in a logical, efficient manner. You can help at home by showing your child how to break multistep and long-term assignments into smaller, more manageable chunks. For example, if your child has three weeks to write a report on his favorite president, you can help him:

1. *Identify* what needs to be done (pick the president; go to the library and get out some books on the person; read the books and take notes; write a first draft; have someone help you edit it; create the final copy).
2. *Write down each step* on a separate slip of paper, and then put the various steps in order.
3. *Group the steps* into manageable chunks.
4. *Set deadlines* for each stage of the project. For example:
    Week 1: choose subject, visit library, read books
    Week 2: create outline, write first draft
    Week 3: get help with editing, produce final copy.
    If necessary, be even more specific. For example:
    Week 1: Monday—choose subject
            Tuesday—visit library
            Wednesday to Friday—read books.
5. *Complete each step* according to the schedule. If necessary, offer small rewards (a game of Monopoly with you; an extra half hour before bedtime one night; a video) for meeting each of the mini-deadlines.

This same approach can be used for nonacademic challenges, such as organizing a collection or planning a birthday party.

What Else Can You Do?

Anything that requires preplanning or categorizing will help build organizational skills. For example, you could:

- *Assign sorting and categorizing chores.* Even house cleaning and food shopping require preplanning and organizing. So give your child responsibility for little sorting jobs that need to be done regularly (such as putting away his own laundry or grocery items; emptying the dishwasher; organizing his bottle cap or rock collection; putting away toys). Or, ask him to help you put together a photo album or scrapbook, clean out a closet, or organize the sports equipment in the garage.

- *Maintain a family calendar.* Hang a big, office-size planning calendar in the kitchen and have everyone in the family write down their daily deadlines and commitments. Refer to the calendar when discussing family outings, play dates, homework, errands, and other plans.

- *Develop checklists.* If your child is having trouble remembering a routine, help him identify the various steps involved and create a checklist. For example, the "Before leaving for school" checklist might include:
    - make up bed
    - brush teeth
    - put lunch or lunch money into backpack
    - make sure homework and school books are in the backpack

- check calendar to remind yourself of after-school commitments
- turn off lights.

- *Cook with your child.* The process of reading a recipe, gathering ingredients, and following directions is a perfect template for approaching any task in an organized manner. Meal planning also requires organizational skills, so you could get your child involved with developing the weekly menu, too.

Other Important Subjects

All of them. Reading, of course, is still of primary importance, since it's the key that unlocks all learning. But every other subject commands attention now. Here are some highlights.

Reading

Your child should be able to pick up a newspaper or a grade-level book and be able to read and understand most of it (not including technical terms or jargon). But teachers admit there is still a wide span in reading by fourth grade. Some students may be reading at a first grade level, while others may be at a sixth grade level or beyond.

The children reading below grade level should be getting extra help. Otherwise, the goal is to continue building reading skills and a love for reading.

Critical Thinking

Teachers still read aloud to fourth graders and use many tools and techniques to build vocabulary, comprehension, and fluency. Some require fourth graders to read as much as a book a week (or an equivalent number of chapters in a lengthier book), and produce some type of oral, written, or three-dimensional evidence (such as a book report, skit, diorama, mobile, poster, or book jacket) that they've read the book and understand it.

Fourth graders are also expected to probe more deeply into what they read—answering questions like: "How are the characters different from each other?"; "If they made different choices, how might the ending be different?"; "Can you think of other books you've read where the characters faced a similar dilemma?"; and "What would you do if you were in the same situation as the lead character?" Class discussions may also explore the story's structure, the cause-and-effect relationships in the text, and the differences between fact and fiction.

Your child will still take regular trips to the school library, and reading will be integrated into science, social studies, and math lessons. Reading at home will also be stressed, as will reading with an adult.

Writing/English

With everything from term papers to college applications looming ahead, writing gets a big push in fourth grade. In many classrooms, it's done on a daily basis. There's usually more written homework, including longer research papers (three to four pages long, with illustrations and at least three outside sources); more rough drafts and editing; and more types of writing assigned, from poetry to news writing to prose. By now, you should also be looking for final drafts with grammar, punctuation, and spelling mistakes corrected.

Special attention this year often goes to perfecting the paragraph. At the beginning of the year, for instance, the class might spend a lot of time dissecting paragraphs, to get a feel for what they are. Then the teacher might focus on one component—such as the opening sentence—and have the children practice it. Once that's mastered, she might move on to supporting sentences, and then finally to concluding sentences. Then the class might put it all together and practice writing full paragraphs.

Writing for Reasons

Fourth grade teachers also strive to showcase the various purposes of writing, from explaining to describing, persuading, entertaining, teaching, listing, and expressing feelings and opinions. Most assignments are still based on specific instructions, such as: "Take off your right shoe and write about it" or "Explain how you got the answer to this math problem." But students are pushed to make their writing more descriptive, less repetitive, and more grammatically correct.

Writing assignments are also designed to help fourth graders practice taking notes, organizing information, paraphrasing, and using reference materials. And, again, there's a great deal of emphasis on editing and revising. Teachers want children to understand that a piece of writing rarely just happens: You have to work on it.

By now, most writing assignments are done in cursive, though printing may be acceptable for a first draft or a special project; the teacher may also allow a final draft to be done on computer.

Communicating

Speaking (and listening) skills are encouraged in a variety of ways, from grouping students in teams and challenging them to find a solution to a problem to having children present oral reports on books they've read, experiments they've done, or problems they've solved. There may also be opportunities for dramatic presentations.

For instance, every year in Frances Sergi's fourth grade, the students celebrate Halloween by dressing up as historic figures and introducing themselves (telling who they are and what they're famous for) to an audience of parents, administrators, other teachers, and peers. During the year, the children are divided into news teams that scour newspapers for current events and then present mock newscasts for their classmates.

Math

Fourth graders go deeper—into long division, fractions, two- and three-digit multiplication, decimals, averaging, perimeter, and area. Some even delve into probability. Problem-solving is still a major focus, with the emphasis on learning *when* and *how* to use the various operations, as well as calculators, graphs, and other tools. Teachers still stress that there are many different ways to find solutions to any given problem.

There's also still a push to make sure children realize that math is part of everyday life. Children talk about the graphs they find in newspapers, for instance. They look at cereal box ingredients to explore the concept of percentages, and they solve word problems that require counting money, estimating costs, and figuring out sales tax and tips.

Encouraging Progress

Though teachers still use manipulatives to introduce and reinforce math concepts, fourth graders are expected to do more math in their heads. "We want children to visualize numbers in their heads, the way good readers make mental pictures from words," explains Lori Murakami, an assessment specialist with the San Francisco Unified School District in California.

However, as in reading, the range of abilities is broad in fourth grade. Some children can't add 7 + 8 in their heads, while others can add or subtract a string of numbers without even picking up a pencil.

If your child isn't yet adept at adding, subtracting, and multiplying, she may complain that math is "too hard" this year, or "too boring." As Murakami points out, "This is the grade when a lot of kids—especially girls and minorities—give up on math. They think that since they don't know their multiplication tables, or they still have to count on their fingers, they're no good at it. In reality, they just need more exposure and hands-on practice."

So don't buy into your child's complaints by saying things like "I was lousy at math, too" or "Just pass the test and you won't have to worry about it ever again." Instead, talk to your child about how everyone learns math in different ways and at different rates. Reassure her that if she keeps working at it, she'll improve. And talk to the teacher about ways you can help your child practice and strengthen her basic math skills at home.

If your child is way ahead of her classmates in math, ask the teacher what you (and she) can do to make the subject more challenging. Sometimes teachers will allow a brighter child to move ahead in the math textbook, or even move into a fifth grade math class.

Science

In science, fourth graders move from asking "*What* will happen?" to exploring *why* things happen—as in "Why does the earth orbit the sun?" or "Why do bears hibernate in winter?"

The focus is on teaching children how to ask questions and make observations. Teachers want fourth graders to be able to analyze, predict, observe, and think scientifically. And, as in math, they want their students to understand that there is no one right way to find an answer. As Cathy Pihl notes, "Instead of asking my students, 'Did you get the right answer?' I always say, 'That's the answer. Explain how you found it.'"

Your child will be doing more independent reading for science (she may have a textbook), and more research projects and reports. There may also be more tests. While some of the themes your child studies this year may seem familiar (animals, the human body, water cycles), the teacher will expect your child to probe each one in more depth (again, looking at the *whys* as well as the *whats*).

Social Studies

In social studies, fourth graders set their sights beyond their homes and communities. They're encouraged to start reading newspapers to stay on top of current events and to relate more of what they hear and learn to what they already know.

Curriculums vary from school to school, of course, but many fourth graders still study their state's history.

Don't expect your child to be memorizing the state bird and flower, however; she's more likely to be wondering what life was like for the people who settled the state, how your state got along with its neighbors, and how things have changed.

Fourth graders may also look at important events in American history up until the Civil War; the geography of the United States, from the East Coast over to the West; and the different branches of the U.S. government. But every school has its own curriculum and goals, so check with the teacher to find out more on specific topics.

Your child may have a social studies textbook, but chances are it won't be the only source of information. Biographies, fiction and nonfiction books, research materials, and even the Internet will probably be used to enhance your child's exploration of the various topics she studies.

Computer

When the machines are available, computer use is strongly encouraged in fourth grade. Teachers want their students to feel comfortable using the computer for word processing and research. In some schools, keyboarding skills are taught, but not all students have the dexterity and coordination to learn this yet.

If there's classroom access to the Internet, your child will probably need your written permission to log on to it, and only educational sites will be sanctioned. If permission is given, he'll learn how to seek and retrieve information for research purposes. If your child does not have access to a computer in school, you may want to sign him up for a computer class over summer vacation or work with him on your home computer.

Health/Physical Education

There will still be a lot of emphasis on staying healthy and avoiding peer pressure to use cigarettes, drugs, or alcohol. In some schools, there is also discussion about the physical and emotional changes that accompany puberty (though many schools wait until fifth grade for this). Even if they don't openly talk about it, most children, by fourth grade, are soaking up information about sex and development from the media and their peers, anyway. So you may want to consider discussing the "facts of life" at home this year.

In gym, your child may be spending more time and energy on learning about the rules, terminology, and safety issues associated with various team sports.

Fine Arts

Hands-on is still the thrust in art and music, though history and theory may be introduced now. Your child may be reading about famous artists or composers, for instance, or learning about things like perspective, proportion, scale, symmetry, and motion (in art); and harmony, tempo, and notation (in music).

For children who are learning to play an instrument, you may see some great strides this year, thanks to greater coordination and awareness of the music. This is also a wonderful age for trips to museums and tickets to concerts, exhibits, plays, and even operas. Your child may even start wanting to listen to popular music on the radio, now, to keep up with the buzz in the classroom.

Foreign Language

This may be the year your child is introduced to a foreign language. If so, you can expect the focus to be on exposure and fun. The teacher will likely work on building vocabulary, reading, and conversation skills while emphasizing pronunciation and intonation. Your child may also learn about the language's country of origin (i.e., France or Spain) and its culture. Games, songs, foods, and traditions of the country may be enjoyed as part of the learning experience.

Homework—and How to Help

You'll probably notice only minimal changes in the homework routine. Your child may have more of it (forty-five to sixty minutes' worth a night), and it may include more textbook assignments, long-term projects, and reports. But overall, there won't be any huge surprises in what your child must do.

What may surprise you is that he remembers to do it. As Judy Bloom notes, "When my son was in third grade, I really had to nag him to get his homework done. This year, he does it all by himself."

This is one of the biggest benefits of having a child who is more independent and aware. Not all children will be as responsible and committed as Bloom's, of course, but a great many fourth graders are able to recognize that doing or not doing homework affects their learning and their grades. And by now, most of them can remember to do it on their own.

The Parent's Job

If your child needs a little hand-holding at the beginning of the year to get her back into the homework habit, go ahead and give it. Or, if she tends to be forgetful and disorganized, help her develop a checklist or other system, so she can organize and budget her time more wisely. (If you encounter homework resistance, review the guidelines on page 150.)

Otherwise, little by little, try to fade into the background. Learning to take responsibility for getting homework done is an important milestone in your child's life—and at this age, there's no need to delay it.

But don't disappear completely. Ask about homework. Look it over. Help if your child asks. Let her know that you're still very interested in what she does for school.

Exercise Restraint

No matter what, *do not* complete the homework (or the report, or the research, or the project) *for* your child, or you'll rob her of an opportunity to get smarter. The point of homework is not to rack up great grades or impress the teacher, it's to reinforce what's taught in the classroom and help your child learn.

If your child frequently labors over homework assignments or genuinely can't do the work, let the teacher know—and she will handle it.

What to Expect on the Social Scene

A lot more action. This is the year when many parents begin to feel insignificant because their child would rather do something ordinary with a friend than something extraordinary with them. But that doesn't mean socializing with peers is getting easier. It's just becoming more important in children's lives.

The biggest source of stress for many fourth graders is

not feeling accepted. Kids this age can get so wrapped up in their friendships that even minor disputes can interfere with schoolwork.

The Good

On the plus side, fourth graders are becoming more discerning about whom they want to hang out with. They're recognizing themselves as unique individuals, tuning in to the traits they like and don't like in friends and trusting their own instincts more. "In third grade, my son usually just went along with what other kids were doing," notes Judy Bloom. "This year he has stronger opinions, and he's not as interested in being a follower. If he sees behaviors he doesn't like in another child, he's more likely to cool the relationship."

Another positive step is that when they find a friend they like, fourth graders are willing to make more concessions to keep that friend and to work at building loyalty, trust, and intimacy. There is more give-and-take in "best friend" relationships, more sharing of secrets, and more sticking up for each other. These deeper friendships don't always last much longer than a semester or a school year, but they can be more satisfying for a child.

The Bad

What works when kids are one-on-one doesn't always translate in a group situation. Then, the heightened awareness of fourth graders leads mainly to emotional tension. For instance, there's often:

- *A distinct separation of the sexes*—on the bus, on the

playground, in the lunchroom, and at birthday parties. A play date between a girl and boy who share a common interest or have known each other since preschool may work. But in a crowd, it's always boys on one side, girls on the other, and mutual disdain in between.

Of course, when boys are alone, or girls are alone, you can count on hearing lots of talk about who likes whom. Notes get passed around on this topic, and many tears are shed over romances that never actually existed. A pair of more sophisticated fourth graders may boast of being boyfriend and girlfriend, but it doesn't mean they'll be any less likely to avoid each other in public.

- *Arguments galore.* As one teacher notes, "Fourth graders love to argue, and it's usually about the stupidest things—like who's friends with whom, and who's going to sit where at lunch." They also have a hard time letting go. If a kid misses the final goal of a soccer game and makes his team lose, he'll get badgered all day. Girls tend to be worse than boys, teachers say. "The boys will fight it out and get over it," explains Steven Levy, a teacher at the Bowman School, in Lexington, Massachusetts. "But the girls will try to get revenge, or they'll hold a grudge for weeks."

- *Lots of competition.* The art of one-upmanship is practiced daily in most fourth grade classrooms. It's not only about who got the best grade, but who has the best toys, who wears the coolest clothes, who scored the most goals, who has the most friends, who has the most baseball cards (and the best players), and who's wearing the coolest sneakers. Kids this age are driven: They want to be successful, well liked, and competent. And most of all, they want to impress their peers.

A little competition can be a good thing: It can help build motivation, self-esteem, and social skills. Too much, however, has the reverse effect. So if you sense your child can't handle the competition at school (or after school), talk to the teacher. And talk to your child about what winning and losing mean to you.

This is a good time, too, to casually remind your child that you love him no matter what he gets for grades or how many points he scores in a game.

The Ugly

The least attractive of all fourth grade behaviors is the tendency to scapegoat. Children this age are so much more aware—and afraid—of their own weaknesses that they'll sometimes overreact to the perceived weaknesses of their peers. As one teacher explains, "This is the year when any child who stands out as different gets picked on or excluded."

What makes a child stand out? There's no formula. It depends on the chemistry of the class. "I've seen children get ostracized for everything from having red hair and freckles to wearing the wrong clothes or being too fat, too skinny, too dumb, too smart, or too poor," says one teacher.

"They just seem to know who the weak ones are," adds a mother. "Once, when I asked my son why he didn't work with a particular student in his class anymore, he told me that he and the boy 'didn't share the same ideas.' I found out later that the child was having a problem with his eyes and needed an aide to help him in the classroom. None of the kids wanted him as a partner anymore."

Teachers work hard to keep teasing and excluding out of the classroom. But they don't have much influence after the school day ends. That's when it's up to parents to set the tone—by discouraging things like inviting all the girls in the class except one to a birthday party or stepping in when a child is being teased.

Helping Your Child

What if *your* child is the one who comes home crying that "Nobody will play with me" or "Everyone laughs at me"? If it only happens now and then, just be there to listen and reassure your child. If it seems to be a chronic problem, however, you should take action before your child develops lasting scars. Here are some options:

- *Talk to the teacher.* A lot of times, children will keep their cruelest words and actions out of sight of adults, so the teacher may not be aware there's a problem. But once she does know, she can often make adjustments in the classroom—such as switching seats or pairing your child with a more popular kid during a class project—to ease the tension. She may also be able to identify the source of the teasing and talk to the other children about the consequences of their behavior. In some cases, a school counselor can be called in to talk to the entire class about respect and acceptance.

- *Help your child fit in.* If the "cool" look this year

involves jeans and T-shirts, don't send your child to school in a frilly dress or dressy pants and nice shoes. If hair is the issue causing problems, encourage your child to get a cut that's more in fashion. You don't have to force your kid to totally blend in or spend every penny you earn on buying the "right" brands, but if your child is being rejected for something she's willing to change, help her out.

- *Minimize negative habits.* Some children get shut out because they don't bathe frequently enough, or they pick their nose, or they have bad breath. Ask the teacher if these kinds of issues are causing problems for your child and then work together on breaking the bad habits.

    Another possibility is that your child's social skills are lacking. Often children will avoid a classmate who is painfully shy, or overly rude or aggressive, or who can't share, talks out of turn, or is generally disruptive. If this is the case, talk about and model more socially acceptable behaviors. If necessary, ask the school counselor to help.

- *Remind your child of his strengths.* If your child is being teased for things he can't control (his hair color or brain power, for instance), acknowledge the hurt he is feeling, but don't obsess about it. Instead, dwell on subjects he's interested in (football or painting, for instance) and find opportunities to remind him of his strengths ("You really have a special gift for writing stories" or "I'm amazed at how easily you pick up on math"). Sign him up for extracurricular activities that further build his sense of competence. When a child *knows* he's good at something, it's easier for him to cope when other children say mean things.

- *Teach her to stand up for herself.* Shy and passive children are more likely to be teased than those who can confidently say "Leave me alone" or laugh in response to verbal jabs. Talk to your child about different strategies she can use when other kids tease her. For instance, if she usually gets flustered or cries when someone teases her, teach her to hide her emotions and play down her response. Explain that bullies don't think it's much fun to tease someone who doesn't seem to care. Other strategies include:

  - walking away
  - telling a teacher or other adult
  - responding with comments like "I know you are, but what am I?" or "It takes one to know one."

  Ask your child to come up with some ideas; role-play the strategies your child seems to like.

- *Arrange play dates.* Children act differently when they're not part of a large herd. So look for children who share similar interests with your child and invite them over, or take your child and a friend out to the movies, or bowling, or for ice cream.

Battling Peer Pressure

As painful as it is to see your child on the "outs," it can be even more worrisome to see her running with the "in" crowd. Children don't always choose the best role models to follow. As one teacher notes, "The kids who are most looked up to in my class aren't the smart ones who are working hard and cooperating. It's the ones who wear cool clothes and constantly talk back to annoy the teacher." In addition, in some communities, fourth grade is when children get their first real exposure to peers who think it's cool to drink, smoke, or try drugs.

The best way to protect your child from negative peer pressure is to keep the lines of communication open at home. That means looking out for subtle signs that your child is upset about something and asking how she's feeling. It also means taking your child's problems seriously—even if they seem silly to you.

"Fourth graders are going through a lot of changes and have a lot of questions," says Lori Murakami. "They'll still bring them to parents if they think their parents will listen. But if you lecture, laugh, or seem too busy to care, they'll turn to their friends for advice."

It'll also help if you don't overreact when your child makes exploratory statements like "Smoking doesn't seem so bad to me." Instead, calmly give her the facts you know, in a nonthreatening manner. For example, you might say: "Well, studies have shown that smoking damages the heart and the lungs and contributes to many life-threatening conditions such as lung cancer and heart disease. I don't smoke because I don't want those things to happen to my body. And I'd hate to see you harm your good health by smoking."

Now's the time to help your child think through the choices she'll be facing in a few short years.

The After-School Schedule

Another good way to protect your child from caving in to negative peer pressure is to make sure he has one or two after-school activities that he's good at *and* he enjoys.

At any age, the chance to pursue a passion, develop a talent, or engage in an active sport yields many important benefits. It can help a child relax and cope with stresses at school, release pent-up energy and frustration, and discover abilities and interests he never realized he had. In addition, studies have shown that extracurricular activities can boost a child's performance in school and provide weak students with a reason to feel proud and capable.

At this age—when the approval of peers is becoming paramount—it's especially important to help your child feel capable and talented. Children who are really good at something—such as playing a sport or an instrument, doing karate or ballet, or being able to draw—develop stronger self-esteem and often win the respect of their peers.

"My daughter is not part of the 'in' crowd," notes Joan Lenowitz. "But she gets a lot of respect from her classmates because she's the top player on her soccer team. It really makes a difference when a child can excel in an area that's important to her peers."

After-school pursuits can also provide extra time to learn social skills. In fact, if your child is having trouble fitting in at school, a new environment where the other children share a similar interest can turn the popularity problem around.

Keeping It Healthy

Getting a fourth grader to sign up for an activity usually isn't difficult. In fact, most children this age want to do a million things, from ballet to baseball, just to be with their friends or to have a chance to show off their skills.

It's still important to set limits on after-school experiences, however. While most fourth graders have the strength and stamina to do more after school, they also have more homework obligations. Anything that makes your child stay up late in order to get homework done is too much. So set time aside for homework first and then decide what else you can work in.

It's also important to:

- *Let your child choose the activity.* Excelling in an area *you* care about won't benefit your child half as much as doing something *she* cares about. Nor does it help if you sign your child up for a class or a sport just because her friends are in it. That might have been okay in preschool, but at this stage it's not the way to go. Your child is in the process of discovering herself, so in the long run it's better for her to pursue her own interests; she can always use play date time to be with her friends.

- *Keep it low-key.* Too much pressure can turn anything your child loves into a nightmare. And too much "constructive" criticism can convince a child to give up. So if you find yourself (or the coach or the teacher) pushing your child to win or excel rather than play, explore, and have fun, back off or step in.

Children this age are competitive enough without having adults encourage more competition.

Look for activities that enable your child to develop her skills and sportsmanship and help her feel successful. More importantly, monitor your own behaviors, words, and attitudes, to make sure you're not the cause of the pressure.

- *Don't overdo it.* Some children can handle more than others. But nine-year-olds aren't very good at knowing when to stop or cut back. They want to do everything now, and they think they can. You'll know your child is overscheduled if she *frequently*:

  - acts grouchy, mopey, or irritable
  - can't settle down at bedtime
  - picks fights with siblings
  - complains that you're treating her unfairly or don't love her as much as you love her siblings
  - brings home grades that are lower than what you know she's capable of earning
  - has trouble getting homework done on time
  - starts overeating
  - veges out in front of the TV
  - complains of stomachaches, headaches, or mysterious illnesses.

  If you notice these or other signs of stress, reconsider her entire schedule and build a new one that's less demanding.

- *Save time for the family.* Just because your child *wants* to spend every minute of the weekend with her best friend doesn't mean you should let her. Growing up is so much more complicated today, and families don't have as much time to spend together as in the past. But just being around a parent—even doing boring things like food shopping, chores, or errands—is extremely instructive for a child. By watching how you behave in various situations, your child picks up on your deepest values (about what's most important in life and how other people should be treated, for instance). She also learns important life skills (how to run a household, budget money, plan meals, and so on).

One-on-one play time is important, too, because it teaches your child that you care enough to spend your limited time focusing on her, and it opens the door to relaxed communication. You may find out more about what's happening in school when you and your child are playing a board game together, reading a book before bedtime, or enjoying an afternoon out, than when you drill her after school each day.

If you think you're too busy, or keep telling yourself that you'll catch up with your child later—when things calm down—you may miss out. The teenage years are approaching quickly.

By the time your child reaches fifth grade, that first day of kindergarten may seem like something that happened a long time ago, in somebody else's life. You may even find it amusing to think about the feelings and fears you had back then, when your child seemed so small and vulnerable.

Now, instead of worrying "Will my child cry when I drop her off at school?" and "Will she ever learn to read?" you've moved on to bigger issues: "Will she have a good teacher?"; "Will she get good grades?"; "Will she find a best friend?"

This year, your concerns may deepen. Your child is no longer a single-digit person (a seven-, eight-, or nine-year-old); she's moving into the double digits (ages ten and eleven), when preadolescence officially begins. As Becky Laurin, a mother of three, notes, "Fifth graders today look and act much older than we did in fifth grade.

We were still just babies at age ten. But they're already moving into puberty and starting to think about dating and cliques and adolescent kinds of things."

They're also shouldering a heavier workload at school. More is expected in terms of what they learn and how much they need to know. As one teacher admits, "The fifth grade curriculum is much more difficult now than when I first started teaching fourteen years ago. In math, for example, I'm introducing material to fifth graders that *I* didn't even learn until high school. In some ways, it's good, because the students seem ready for it," she adds. "But it's much harder today to be a straight A student."

ANTICIPATE UPS AND DOWNS

Understanding that your child's fifth grade experience may be quite different from yours is an important first step in making this a successful school year. It's also important to prepare yourself for some ups and downs in behavior.

In some ways, your child will seem quite young. He may still enjoy playing with toys you consider babyish, for example. Or he may still cry when he's stressed over a test or things don't work out quite the way he planned. He may even send out signals, now and then, that he could really use a cuddle or a hug.

But you'll also see more of those teenage-like behaviors, such as moodiness, defiance, and obsession with peers. Your child will become more analytical as time goes by and eventually begin comparing your lifestyle choices to those of the parents of her peers. Even teachers get a closer look this year. As one parent notes, "Fifth grade is when my child stopped automatically loving her teacher. Instead of hearing 'My teacher says this' and 'My teacher thinks that' all the time, I now get 'My teacher is so boring' or 'My teacher is unfair.'"

Judging adults more harshly is a natural part of the separation process your child is about to begin. As Becky Laurin notes, "This age is a lot like the toddler years. That old 'I need you, but get away from me' attitude is back."

Your Chance to Practice

Keeping your balance, and knowing when to hold back and when to hug, won't be easy this year. But try to think of it as good training. As one father with junior high–age kids notes, "Fifth grade is merely a preview of what lies ahead."

The most important thing you can do is keep the lines of communication open and be there for your child. "Fifth grade is a really special year," says Kathy Hoekenga, of Trinity School, in Menlo Park, California, "because it marks the end of childhood." It may be the last year when your child really wants you to be involved in the classroom or to chaperone school field trips. So it's important to do whatever you can—take time off from work or cut back on your own schedule, for instance—to attend school events, help out in the classroom, and spend one-on-one time with your child.

What Fifth Graders Are Like

They're old pros. They know the school routine, and they know what it means to study. They still like to learn, and they have a lot more to say. But those preadolescent hormones are beginning to kick in, and they're definitely becoming more daring about questioning adults and expressing their own opinions. As Donna Hupe, a teacher at Haine Middle School, in Cranberry Township, Pennsylvania, puts it, "By fifth grade, children are beginning to look across at the adults in their lives, instead of up to us."

Different children mature at different rates, of course. And factors like where you live and what your child is allowed to watch on TV will influence how quickly he adopts adolescent-like behaviors. But at some point in fifth grade, you'll probably notice a variety of changes.

Physical Changes

Puberty is approaching. How close your child is to actually experiencing it will depend on his or her particular pattern of growth. But in general, between the ages of ten and eleven, girls begin to experience:

- a spurt in growth and an increase in weight
- the beginnings of breast development
- some appearance of pubic hair
- a vaginal discharge (or even menstruation).

Boys tend to develop more slowly, but around age eleven you may see:

- a rapid gain in height and weight
- a rounding of body contours
- an enlargement of the testicles and scrotum
- some emergence of pubic hair.

The earlier bloomers are bound to feel self-conscious about their new bodies. They may be more clumsy, due to an unevenness in growth, and feel more awkward, since they can't quite make their bodies behave as they used to. Girls who are physically advanced may feel confused by and uncomfortable about the sexual attention or teasing they receive from classmates and older males. And children of both sexes may get excluded over issues like height, weight, and body odor. (Though most ten-year-olds are well aware of what soap, toothpaste, and deodorant are for, few children this age seem to have the desire to use them.)

The late bloomers are bound to feel self-conscious, too, since they can see that some of their classmates are getting closer to being grown-up (at least physically) than they are. They don't want to be left behind, and they don't want to feel in any way different, so they tend to worry and obsess. For girls the leading question is: Will I ever grow breasts? For boys: How can I get some muscles?

Reassuring Words

No matter where your fifth grader falls in rate of development, it's important to be sensitive to how he feels about his body. Try to avoid any comments, no matter how harmless they may seem, because they'll likely touch a raw nerve in your child's preadolescent psyche. Even something as innocent as "Boy, you've gotten big!" can be interpreted by an insecure fifth grader to mean "Wow, look how fat and ugly you are."

"Children this age operate under a strange paradox," notes Janet Schwartz, a mother of two. "They are more aware of the world and what's happening around them. But at the same time, they're more convinced than ever that everyone is noticing and judging them." So every little comment gets microscopic attention.

A better approach is to talk to your child about puberty, give her books on the subject, and reassure her with facts when insecure comments slip out. For instance, if your daughter complains that she's the only girl in the class who doesn't need a bra, or if your son is despondent because his arms are still skinny, you can explain: "All children mature at different rates. I know it's hard to be patient. But you can be sure that, with time, your body will begin to look more like your friends'."

More importantly, instead of dwelling on weight and appearance, stress the importance of getting lots of exercise and eating nutritious foods to build a body that's strong and healthy.

Emotional Changes

For the most part, fifth graders are fairly easy to be around. They're competent, friendly, and self-reliant. They have good self-control and a well-developed sense of humor. And they're interested in a lot of the same subjects adults are.

But they aren't quite as consistent. So don't be surprised if your normally calm and easygoing child has an unexpected meltdown over something as simple as a change in plans. For example, if you say "By the way, honey, we're going food shopping at eleven A.M. today, instead of ten," your child may lash out with "What? I can't believe it. How could you ruin my whole day? I never get to do *anything* I want."

You should also prepare for more:

- *defiance* ("No way! I'm not cleaning that up because it's not my mess. You do it!")

- *embarrassment* ("I can't go to school with this haircut! Everyone will laugh!")
- *hurt feelings* ("Everyone says I'm fat" or "Everyone got invited except me")
- *accusations of unfair behavior* ("You *always* side with her, and you *never* listen to me!")
- *distancing* ("Do you have to come with me, Mom? Can't you just let me off at the corner?")
- *distraction* ("Well, I started to pick up my room, but then I found this book and started reading it..." or even "I did clean my room: I just didn't notice all those dirty clothes in the corner")
- *sudden shifts in mood* (thanks to the flood of hormones in your child's developing body, combined with her newfound quest for independence and her growing desire to fit in with her peers).

Even if your child is on the younger, less-developed side of fifth grade, chances are she'll feel the fallout from her classmates. "Fifth grade is when my daughter's best friend started her period and began acting moody and emotional," notes one mother. "She'd be her usual friendly self one day, and the next she'd be saying mean things to hurt my daughter's feelings. We spent a lot of time that year talking about her friend's behavior."

Falling in Love

Another inevitable effect of the hormone surge is a heightened interest in the opposite sex. While some children in the class will still be at the "All boys [or girls] have cooties" stage, others will be veering off to romance-land. There will probably be at least a few class couples, but for the most part their "dating" will consist of calling each other on the phone, going for walks or bike rides together after school, and possibly going to the movies or the mall with a group of other friends.

"In a class of thirty-five kids, there might be eight or nine with a working knowledge of their body parts," notes Christopher Ageeb, of Colbert Elementary School, in Hollywood, Florida. "But for the most part, fifth grade relationships are fairly innocent. Kids still pass notes saying 'Do you like me? Circle yes or no.'"

Even if you think it's cute that your daughter has a boyfriend (or that your son has a girlfriend), it's best not to encourage unsupervised dating at this stage. Most fifth graders—even those who are physically mature—don't have the emotional maturity to handle a serious boy/girl relationship. Besides, your child isn't even a teenager yet; there's plenty of time ahead for falling in love.

Maintaining Perspective

The good news is that none of these emotional changes is likely to be overwhelming this year: They'll just pop up now and then, to remind you that the teen years are ahead. You still have time to practice survival skills before your child reaches full adolescence.

The best way to respond? With flexibility, and firm but reasonable discipline. Children this young aren't terribly in touch with their feelings, and they don't always know why they act rude or get angry or dissolve into tears over nothing. So it doesn't help to get angry back.

What does help is maintaining a sense of humor. "Kids

this age will say the most outlandish things—like 'You're so mean' or 'I hate you'—just to take a stand or get out of doing a chore," notes Janet Schwartz. "What I usually do is take a deep breath and make my son do it anyway. For example, I'll say, 'You hate me. That's nice. But you still have to brush your teeth.'"

If your child oversteps the boundaries of decency in your household—by swearing, hitting, or throwing things, for instance—you should apply an immediate consequence (such as sending him to his room or removing a privilege), no matter what triggered the outburst. It should be clear that certain behaviors are not tolerated under any circumstances.

Otherwise, try to be flexible. If your child is just being moody or seems genuinely overwhelmed, take the time to find out what's bothering him and let him know you're willing to help. You might say, "You seem really upset today. Did something happen at school?" or "I think that what you're really angry about is the F you got for not handing in your project on time. If you want, I can help you set some deadlines that'll help keep you on schedule with the next project."

Cognitive Changes

Interest in the world expands further in fifth grade, as does media awareness. Children can now tune in to some of the more subtle aspects of books, movies, and television shows; they can pick up on the implications of news reports. There's more depth to their ability to understand, analyze, and compare what they see and hear to what they already know. They aren't terribly skilled at abstract reasoning yet, but they are formulating more targeted questions.

Now, when your child hears a snatch of hot news—about a presidential scandal, a terrorist bombing, or a school shooting, for instance—he's going to want (and need) to know what, when, where, and why it happened. Most of all, he's going to wonder "How will that affect *me*?" When he hears about classmates who are dating, smoking, or experimenting with drugs and alcohol, or when he sees those behaviors glamorized in TV shows and movies, he's going to start asking "What if I made the same choices?"

"With fifth graders, you can't just gloss over the issues," says Donna Hupe. "You need to explain things and talk things over, so they won't feel fearful or helpless."

Fifth graders aren't only trying to make sense of the world, they're trying to figure out where they fit in—and what *they* can do to help. "Fifth graders want life to be fair," says Kathy Hoekenga. "When they hear about things like the Civil Rights Movement, or any other incidents of people being treated unfairly, they pick right up on them and want to take action. They can be quite passionate, now, about the issues they believe in."

Getting Answers

Teachers do what they can to build on fifth graders' curiosity and passion. But there are many lessons about choices and values that are better taught at home. That's why being available and willing to answer your child's questions is extremely important at this stage. Even though your child may not show it, your opinion still carries a lot of weight. And how you react to questions now will set the tone for how the two of you communicate when adolescence sets in.

Also, it's important to realize that fifth graders today are facing choices and pressures many of us parents didn't even know existed at age ten. If you aren't willing to answer your child's questions or listen to her concerns, she's going to go looking for answers elsewhere—namely, from popular culture and her peers. So if you're not sure whether you can find the time to spend with your child, just ask yourself: "Do I want my child to follow *my* advice—or the advice of another ten-year-old?"

Unplanned Moments

That's not to say your fifth grader will be knocking down the door to get your opinion. Remember, children this age are more cautious about believing adults and more willing to challenge a parent's or teacher's authority. They're also less likely to answer a direct question like "Are you okay?" or "Are you worried about something?" Instead, if they have something on their minds, they might act miserable and nasty, they might withdraw to their rooms, or they might just hang around and say nothing.

It's up to you to send out signals that you're ready and willing to talk and listen. Often that involves simply giving your child your full attention during those unplanned moments when she asks for it.

"My daughter, Kathy, tends to keep things to herself until an issue gets really overwhelming," notes Beth Gillespie, a mother of two. "So I usually let her decide when to approach me with questions. She tends to be most talkative when I'm tucking her in at night." Other children tend to open up when their parents are busy reading the newspaper, driving the car, or running errands—in other words, when they know they don't have to make direct eye contact and the adult won't just walk away.

Strategies That Help

No matter when your child chooses to bring up a concern, try to remember that it's more important to listen than to speak. If you react too strongly ("How could you think a thing like that?" or "This is what you have to do..." or "That's ridiculous. Everyone knows that..."), you might scare your child off. Or, she might get frustrated by your response and either roll her eyes or storm out of the room.

In general, you'll have a better chance of finding out what's on your child's mind and getting across your own opinions if you:

- *Allow your child to speak,* even if he's saying something you don't agree with. Children this age are "trying on" a lot of different opinions and ideas; just because they *say* they believe something, it doesn't mean they're committed to it. So try to listen without interrupting.

- *Show your child you've heard what he's said,* either by repeating it back ("So, it sounds like you think it's okay to cheat on a test as long as you don't get caught") or by asking questions ("Why did your friend think he needed to cheat? What did the teacher say? What did you think when you heard about it?").

- *Respond calmly* (even if you're feeling angry, frustrated, or worried inside). And try to avoid telling your child how he *ought* to think or feel. For instance, instead of saying "Cheating is wrong—you should know that by now" or "I think you'd better stop hanging around with that friend!" you might try: "I'm sorry to hear that you feel cheating is okay sometimes. I have to say that I think it is very wrong to cheat on a test. It's unfair to the other students who worked hard on studying. It takes advantage of the teacher's trust. And it robs the person who's cheating of an opportunity to learn...."

Try to remember that the difference between expressing your opinion and lecturing your child lies in your tone of voice and how well you listen. Most of all, don't give up—even if your child resists your interest or offers monotone or nasty responses. Deep down, he still needs you and wants to know what you think—and that you care.

What Fifth Graders Should Know

Even in fifth grade, there's usually a wide span of academic abilities in any given classroom. In reading, for instance, teachers see everything from beginning readers to children who can whiz through junior high books. In writing, there are some fifth graders who can dash off pages of copy, while others are still struggling with basic sentence construction. In math, there's everything from the kid who still doesn't know his times tables to the one who's gliding through the sixth grade textbook.

Ideally, however, fifth grade teachers like to see students who can:

- find and read books on their own, for research and for pleasure
- summarize information from reference materials and other sources
- write a well-organized paragraph, with proper punctuation and grammar
- edit and revise writing assignments
- multiply two- and three-digit numbers comfortably
- divide one-digit numbers and work with fractions, mixed numbers, and common denominators
- use various operations and tools to solve two-step math problems
- form a hypothesis and set up and carry out a scientific experiment
- work on a project independently or as part of a team
- manage time and information well enough to meet homework deadlines.

Strength in the basic skills—reading, writing, math, and research—is especially important, since fifth grade is another one of those years when lots of new material is introduced. But most teachers also look for a positive attitude toward learning. As Margot Sawicki, a teacher at P.S. 101, in Forest Hills, New York, remarks, "The desire to learn is what's most important. No matter where a child's skills are at the start of the year, if you can spark her interest and build her self-confidence, you can see amazing progress in fifth grade."

Children Who Aren't Ready

At this stage, schools are usually reluctant to hold children back because it can have an impact on self-esteem.

However, teachers say you should be concerned about your child's ability to keep up in fifth grade if he:

- seems significantly less mature (physically and/or emotionally) than his classmates
- is reading way below grade level
- still writes in a disorganized manner, without regard to punctuation and grammar
- has not been able to memorize his times tables.

These are all red flags that your child needs some sort of extra help, whether it's a tutor, a remedial class at school, or a repeat of fourth grade. Talk to your child's teacher or the school's principal or counselor to find out what the options are and which of the available strategies would best suit your child.

What to Expect in the Classroom

More of the same. Fifth grade classrooms usually don't differ significantly from fourth grade rooms. And the daily schedule will probably be similar. You'll still see a combination of independent and group work; lots of integration among subjects (using writing in math lessons, for instance, and reading books for social studies); and movement to other classrooms for lessons with specialist teachers (in reading, math, science, art, music, or a foreign language, for instance).

What may seem most different is your child's motivation level. While fifth graders tend to be ready, willing, and able to learn, they don't always lap up whatever the teacher introduces the way younger children do. There are more facts and skills they *have* to memorize now, the work is getting harder, and they have more responsibility for their own learning—even when the lessons are not much fun.

Plus, they're at an age when questioning and testing are natural. So they're more likely to strike a skeptical pose when new material is introduced ("Why should I have to learn this?") or to complain about school and homework ("It's too boring!").

Maintaining Motivation

The best teachers will try any strategy they can think of to keep students interested and motivated in fifth grade. That includes letting students work together on assignments; assigning creative, hands-on book projects instead of just written reports; using games and activities to introduce new information; and allowing children to pick their own subjects for major research reports. As Margot Sawicki notes, "It's not enough to cram their heads with knowledge. You have to spark their desire to keep on learning."

You can help at home in a number of ways. For example:

- *Notice your child's strengths, instead of her weaknesses.* Rather than dwell on the bad grade she got on the social studies test, comment on the good grades she got in math and science (then offer to help her study for the next social studies exam). Show her you value her hard work and effort by hanging up some of her best—or most improved—work at home. Talk about the qualities you see in her that make her special ("You have a real gift for making other people smile"; "I'm proud of the way you work hard to get the best grades you can"; "I love the way you blend so many different colors in your artwork"). When children feel they are special in some way, they're more likely to keep trying their best at school.

- *Talk about how perseverance improves performance.* Use yourself as an example ("When I first started playing the piano, I was all thumbs, and I thought I'd never learn. But the more I practiced, the better I became"). Use famous people ("In order to win that gold medal, she had to skate eight hours a day, six days a week, from the time she was seven years old"). Use your child ("Wow. You never thought you'd pass that test, but you studied hard for it and you got an A! What a difference it makes when you put in your best effort").

- *Help your child get organized.* If she's feeling overwhelmed by a long-term or multi-step project, help her sit down and break it into smaller, less intimidating chunks. Talk about how every major accomplishment in life begins with one small step in the right direction.

- *Offer rewards for hard work and improvement.* If your child is having a tough time getting motivated to do rote homework or a major project, use small rewards to get her started ("If you can finish the first draft by Sunday afternoon, I'll take you to the movies"; "For every math problem you do correctly within fifteen minutes, I'll give you an extra minute with the light on at bedtime"). When it comes to praising grades, don't just concentrate on the good ones; let your child know you're most proud of the ones that show improvement (even if she went from a C– to a C+, for instance).

- *Set a good example.* Show your child how much you value education and learning by continuing to read and learn more about your own work or your favorite hobbies. Share the excitement you feel about things you love to do, and if your child seems interested, get her involved, too.

The Most Important Subject This Year

Responsibility. As in fourth grade, all of the academic subjects—from reading and math to social studies and science—are important now. But there's more emphasis than ever on independent learning. As one teacher puts it, "The time for hand-holding is over. Children are now facing middle school and junior high, when they'll be changing teachers and classrooms every period, doing more independent research, and grappling with peer pressure. It's extremely important for them to realize, now, that they're responsible for their own actions." That includes meeting homework deadlines, studying for tests, waiting their turn to speak, and controlling outbursts and aggressive behavior at school.

Teaching responsibility isn't always easy. As Janet Schwartz notes, "Fifth graders hate to take any kind of personal responsibility. If something goes wrong, it's always someone else's fault. For instance, if my son's team loses a baseball game, I'll hear things like 'I would have hit that ball if he had thrown a better pitch' or 'We could have won if so-and-so hadn't dropped that fly ball in the second inning' all day long."

Reinforcing Responsible Behavior

Most fifth grade teachers realize they have their work cut out for them. So they use lots of different strategies to reinforce the idea that each child is in control of his or her own behavior. And they stress that different behaviors have different consequences—so it pays to think before you act.

For example, your child may encounter:

- *Varied deadlines for homework and projects.* This year there may be daily, weekly, bimonthly, and monthly homework deadlines for your child to keep track of—and meet.

- *Stricter deadlines for homework and projects.* Many fifth grade teachers have a "no excuses accepted" policy—and will stick to it even if parents try to intervene (unless, of course, there's an emergency involved).

- *A "find your own answers" policy.* There's a big push in this grade to train kids to find answers on their own. So many fifth grade teachers make it their mission to answer students' questions with their own questions. For instance, if a child says, "I can't figure out this math problem. Can you help me?" the teacher won't say, "You did this wrong" or "Here's the right answer." He'll say, "Explain to me what you did to get this far. Now, what do you think should happen next? What do you need to do to make that happen?"

- *Team projects.* By working together in a group, children learn to divide and share responsibility. It also helps them see how their actions can directly help or hinder the performance of others.

- *A step-by-step discipline system.* For example, in Christopher Ageeb's classroom, if a child breaks a rule—by picking on a classmate, for instance—he might first get a warning. If he does it again, he gets a "busy work" assignment or has to write in a behavior journal. If he violates the rule a third time, he gets detention. For a fourth infraction, he spends time with the principal.

  "At every step, I emphasize to the child that he has a choice," says Ageeb. "He can either follow the rule or suffer the consequences of the next stage of discipline."

  The key, say teachers, is to be strict and consistent, especially during the first few months of school. Otherwise, as Ageeb puts it, "you're meat for the rest of the year."

- *Rewards for good behavior.* Some teachers make their students "earn" their recess every day, by cooperating and behaving in class. Others keep behavior charts and will give out small rewards, such as a piece of candy for no infractions, on a weekly basis. Others will hand out points that can be accumulated and applied toward a bigger reward, such as eating lunch in the classroom; having an in-class bagel or pizza party; or buying merchandise in a school store. In some classrooms, the students can pool their good behavior points and put them toward a big end-of-the-year party. Whatever the reward, the goal is to get students to recognize that good behavior has consequences, too—pleasant ones.

- *Impromptu conversations.* As Margot Sawicki points out, "Not a day goes by when there isn't some problem in the classroom that's related to being responsible and treating other people with respect." For example, one child might walk down the aisle and bump into another kid's desk, causing a pencil to fall off. So the teacher has to stop and say, "Something fell down when you walked by her desk. What's the right thing to do when that happens?" The need for repetition never ends.

- *Community service.* With their energy and budding idealism, fifth graders are perfect candidates for helping others. In school, they might be encouraged to tutor their peers, read to younger students, or help with setup and cleanup for school events. Teachers may also encourage them to write letters to promote world peace, raise money to help a charity, sponsor a needy child, or sing holiday songs at a nursing home.

  It's important to support the school in its efforts to make your child more responsible. In fact, there's no reason not to, since responsible children make life at home easier, too.

Other Important Subjects

All of the major subjects get their share of attention this year. While the overall goals for each one don't change, there is new material to learn. So your child may feel this school year is "harder."

Here's a quick look at what to expect.

Reading

The main goals are the same as in previous school years. To:

- move weaker readers ahead (preferably to grade level, but any improvement is laudable)
- build vocabulary and comprehension, so all of the students can read more complex texts
- increase exposure to different genres (mysteries, fantasies, poetry, plays, biographies, historical fiction, and so forth)
- sharpen literary criticism skills
- turn every child into a person who loves to read *something*.

Most fifth grade teachers require oral or written book reports or projects every couple of weeks. There are frequent trips to the library, there is lots of literature in the classroom, and fiction and nonfiction books (and textbooks) are used to enhance learning in every single subject.

Writing

The overall goal is to get children to write as much as they can, at whatever level they can. Some children may still need special help with basic sentence construction or paragraph writing. But the majority of fifth graders work on:

- taking notes
- summarizing and paraphrasing information from various reference sources
- improving grammar and spelling
- sharpening word choices and adding details to improve clarity and description
- honing their ability to write a clear beginning, mid-

dle, and end—in both creative and expository writing assignments

- practicing speech writing, persuasive writing, creative writing, and other forms of written communication
- applying their writing skills to math, science, social studies, and even art and music lessons
- practicing the major stages of producing a piece of written work: outlining, writing, editing, and revising.

The Big Push

Many teachers really push writing in fifth grade, because their students must take a standardized writing test in sixth grade. (Schools have different schedules for standardized tests, however, so check with the teacher to find out what your child will be facing.) There may be daily writing workshops, when children read and critique each other's writing or work on editing and revising; time for daily journal writing; and weekly at-home writing assignments.

In some fifth grade classrooms, children also learn, step-by-step, how to produce a five- to twelve-page research report, complete with outside sources, charts, and illustrations. One week, the teacher might talk about how to pick a topic and then narrow it down. Subsequent lessons might focus on steps like finding information, taking notes, creating an outline, writing an opening paragraph, and so on. Once all the steps have been covered and practiced, the children pick their own topic to research and spend the next grading period working through each of the steps they learned about.

Again, it's all meant to prepare them for the academic work that lies ahead.

Math

Many children—even those who usually love math—find it tough this year because there's a lot of new material that's fairly rote and complex. After the initial review period, for example, fifth graders often dive into:

- computations with fractions and mixed numbers
- long division
- decimals
- statistics
- geometry
- probability
- the metric system.

A strong grasp of addition, subtraction, and multiplication is essential at this point. Children who aren't yet caught up in these basic skills will probably be placed in a separate math group and receive special instruction. Advanced math students may be given higher level work or be allowed to join a sixth grade math class (or work with a sixth grade textbook).

Attention is still given to manipulatives and problem solving. And teachers still want their students to feel that the math they're learning extends beyond the textbook. "Whenever I can, I try to relate the math the kids are learning to real life," says Elizabeth Perkins, of Arcanum Elementary School, in Arcanum, Ohio. "For instance, I might have them figure out a budget to keep a rock band on the road or raise money to make a music video. Or I'll have them practice working with percentages by looking at newspaper ads and figuring out how much they'd pay in interest to buy a new car or home. It makes math seem more real to them."

Science

Teachers are still training their students to think like little scientists and to use basic inquiry skills (asking, observing, recording, analyzing data, and drawing conclusions) to find answers to scientific questions. There may be a science textbook and/or workbook, but the emphasis should still be on hands-on activities and experiments. For example, when studying chemistry, the students might be asked to construct models of molecules using clay and marshmallows. When studying habitats, they might set up terrariums in the classroom. There may even be activities involving microscopes and test tubes.

Fifth graders also get frequent opportunities to test their own theories by designing and carrying out their own controlled experiments.

What should be different this year is the depth of the inquiries. Fifth graders tend to study both physical science (electricity, magnets, atoms, molecules, and chemistry) and earth (or life) science (environments, weather, water cycles, habitats, food chains). They may cover subjects they've studied before, but they'll go deeper into the terminology and be expected to remember more of the information they learn for tests.

Fifth graders are also encouraged to relate more of what they learn and observe in science lessons to everyday events in their lives. When Perkins's class studied water purification, for instance, they also discussed water-related issues—such as erosion, drainage, and water testing—that were affecting their local community.

Health

Either as part of their scientific studies, or as part of their health curriculum, fifth graders learn more about the human body—including the skeleton, cardiac system, skin, nutritional needs, food sources, and so on. The effects of smoking, alcohol, and drugs on the body are discussed, as is the importance of standing up to peer pressure.

This is also the year in most schools when discussions about puberty occur. Usually, toward the middle or end of the year, the boys and girls get split into separate groups to learn about what puberty is and what kinds of changes to expect—both physically and emotionally—when it begins. Instructors may also talk about sex organs, reproduction, and AIDS (though the details on intercourse are usually left for parents to teach).

In many schools, parents must sign a permission slip to allow their children to receive sex education. But most teachers are strongly in favor of it. As one teacher—who has found condoms in his fifth graders' desks—points out, "A lot of parents don't realize that by fifth grade, children are already soaking up information about sex from their peers and from the media. They don't always get the right information, however, and they don't always understand what they hear. The boys, especially, are starting to trade sexual jokes and limericks, and they may be using sexual words inappropriately, to tease their female classmates. They need to learn now what the words really mean, and why sexual harassment is wrong."

Social Studies

The focus in many fifth grades is on American history. But instead of learning about isolated events, children begin to learn how one event led to another. There may be a time line in the classroom, as well as frequent lessons on U.S. geography. And your child will likely be encouraged to look beyond his textbook to historical fiction, biographies, diaries, maps, and newspaper accounts to find out more about the people and events of different time periods.

There may also be field trips to local historical sites and museums and themed celebrations at school. In Kathy Hoekenga's classroom, for instance, the children have a Colonial Day when they all dress up in period costumes and then play Colonial-era games, make crafts, and share their knowledge of the period. They even reenact a typical old-time school day.

Fifth graders also continue to study the people, geography, and histories of other areas in the Western Hemisphere. They learn about tolerance and respect. They polish their map-reading and research skills. And they learn to think of historical figures as real people—and of themselves as people who are making history.

Special Subjects

As in past years, fifth graders also receive instruction in computer use, art, music, physical education, and sometimes a foreign language. The focus and amount of time spent on these subjects vary from school to school, depending on budgetary and other concerns. But what's most important for parents to know is that all of these subjects are still extremely important. If your child is not being exposed to them in school, make sure her after-school schedule includes opportunities to create, move, and use technology.

Homework—and How to Help

There's more of it (one to two hours a night in some schools). It may be more varied (with daily, weekly, and monthly assignments, for instance). And it'll probably be harder than ever. But the good news is, you're officially off the hook when it comes to making sure it gets done.

Once your child has agreed on a time and place to do her homework each day, you can sit back and relax. Ask about it now and then; make sure your child has all the materials she needs, including library books for research assignments; and be ready to help if your child requests it—but don't get any more involved unless absolutely necessary. Homework is your child's responsibility now. If she doesn't do it, she should suffer the consequences.

Don't Overdo It

Parents who help too much—because they're afraid their child will get a bad grade or get shown up by classmates, or because the child doesn't want to do the work and *begs* for help—are the bane of existence for most teachers. So if you get the urge to correct your child's mistakes, make his lopsided project look better, or fix his sentences so they sound smoother, try to resist. Or, if you find yourself staying up late on a Thursday night, frantically typing your child's last-minute attempt at a research report, make an effort to break the habit—even if you "only want the best" for your child.

Remind yourself that fifth grade teachers expect fifth grade work, and that the purpose of homework is to help your child learn—and to help the teacher know what needs to be taught. When you do the homework or help too much, no one benefits, least of all your child. As one teacher points out, "It's important for children to feel respected for the work they're capable of doing. If the parent 'improves' a project or piece of writing, the child doesn't gain any sense of accomplishment or pride."

Don't Underdo It

The other thing teachers don't like is parents who aren't involved at all. It's one thing to encourage your child to be responsible for homework, and another thing to act like it (or your child) doesn't exist. There is no harm in asking "So, what do you have to do for homework tonight?" Nor is it a crime to help your child organize his time when there's a long-term project; drive him to the local library, so he can find the books he needs for a research paper; quiz him before a big test; remind him of his deadlines; or add a helping hand to a three-dimensional project—as long as your child is clearly the person in charge, and you're just the helper.

As one teacher notes, "Even if you casually ask about homework, and your child merely mumbles a one-word reply, it will make him feel good just to know that you care."

If There Are Problems

As in past years, if homework becomes a battleground, talk to the teacher rather than continue the fight. The work may be too hard for your child; he may need help adjusting his homework routine; or he may just need to learn that life is full of things you have to do that you don't really want to. This is a good time for a child to learn that: From now until college graduation, homework is only going to get harder.

Measuring Progress

The biggest source of stress for many fifth graders is grades. Children who were excellent students in the primary years can't always keep up their high marks in the intermediate period. The work gets harder and requires different kinds of academic strengths.

Unfortunately, by now kids are well aware of the difference between an A and a B or a C and a D. And they know who in the class is getting what. In addition, as junior and senior high school loom—and college hovers in the background—they're becoming more aware of the importance of a good report card. So they're more likely to feel that anything less than perfect is a failure.

But fifth graders are really still too young to be worrying about perfect performance or judging themselves based on a piece of paper with letters on it. So try not to apply too much pressure on your child when it comes to grades.

A Positive Approach

If you notice an obvious slip in your child's grades, talk to the teacher. It might signal an underlying problem, such as teasing from classmates, a friendship that's gone sour, an overwhelming daily schedule, too much pressure to perform, or work that's too difficult.

Otherwise, when a report card comes home:

- *Look for progress, not perfection.* Instead of commenting on the grades (whether they're good or bad), talk about the progress they represent ("Wow! I can see that all that extra studying you did in social studies really paid off").

- *Listen to your child's reaction.* She might be surprised by her grades, they might confirm what she already knows, or she may be puzzled because one or two are lower than expected. Use her comments as a launch pad for determining ways to help her improve ("It sounds like you think you could do better in math. Maybe I can help you think of some ways to sharpen your multiplication and division skills").

- *Separate grades from self-worth.* If your child is in tears because her best friend got a better report card, or she's "only a C student," reassure her that report cards are not measures of self-worth. They're merely tools schools use to let students and parents know how a child is progressing—and they're even limited in their ability to do that. Talk about your child's other gifts and nonacademic accomplishments to help her see that she's a well-rounded person with strengths and weaknesses, just like everyone else. Also, if necessary, let her know that a C isn't a sign of failure: It's an indication that she's doing the same level of work that most fifth graders do.

- *Don't punish your child for bad grades.* If she's been slacking off, the grade itself is punishment enough. If she's been working hard and still can't pull an A or a B, it's not going to help her self-esteem or motivation level to be punished. Instead, look for ways to strengthen her study skills. Get the teacher involved, so your child will know that everyone believes she can do better—and is willing to help. Tell her directly that "doing her best" is more important to you than getting a perfect report card. When children feel they can never live up to their parents' expectations or that no matter what they do it'll never be good enough, they often stop trying.

- *Don't overreact to high grades.* You may be bursting with pride, but if you pin too much importance on those A's, your child may begin to think you value the grades more than what he's learned. In addition, if grades are all you talk about, he'll begin to think that's all you care about—and then lower grades will make him feel like a failure. Instead, express your pride in terms of: "You must have really learned a lot this year" or "Congratulations! I can see that you're working really hard and learning a lot at school."

What to Expect on the Social Scene

Lots of growing pains. Children this age are experiencing so many changes, it's inevitable. Just look at the list:

- Their bodies are growing and changing, making them feel awkward and self-conscious.
- Their hormones are changing, causing feelings and mood swings they don't understand (not to mention new experiences like menstruation and perspiration).
- Their relationships are changing. The opposite sex is looking more attractive, friendships are solidifying into cliques, and group sleepovers and get-togethers are becoming major social events—to be invited to or excluded from.
- Their interest in peers is growing, and they're becoming more engrossed in discussing who's pretty, who's powerful, and who's popular.
- Their pecking order is changing, and there's more fighting (usually physically among boys and verbally among girls), more jealousy, and more hurt feelings as kids vie for power and status.

- They're facing more pressure to "fit in" by following negative behaviors such as smoking, swearing, teasing other kids, or cheating.
- Their awareness of the material world is growing, and having the right clothing, footwear, hairstyles, and "stuff" is becoming just as important as having the "right" friends.

If you think back to how you felt in about seventh grade, you might get a glimpse of the emotional turbulence your fifth grader is (or will soon be) feeling.

Stay Calm

The best thing you can do, at this point, is *expect* to see peer problems. That way, you won't overreact if your child starts avoiding the friends she's had since preschool or comes home crying because her best friend joined a new clique or she didn't get invited to the "in" sleepover. As one teacher notes, "Parents are constantly getting upset about how other people's kids behave. They think everything would be fine if only that other child didn't do this or say that. But it's usually not true. All children are involved in peer conflicts at this point."

As painful as rejection and teasing can be for your child—as well as for you—they're a normal part of growing up. And they can actually teach children lessons about getting along, accepting others, and accepting one's self.

So instead of becoming indignant or rushing to pick up the phone and complain when another child, says something mean or does something cruel to your child, remind yourself that fifth graders are still in the process of maturing. They aren't supposed to be great at getting along yet. If you take their behaviors too seriously, you'll simply add fuel to the fire.

The Real Story

Besides, there's always a chance that your child isn't telling you the whole story. Maybe the reason she wasn't invited to the sleepover was because she called the girl who was hosting it a snob. Or maybe her best friend isn't calling the house anymore because your child has been snubbing her at school. When there's trouble afoot, most children don't want to admit that they're part of the problem, because they don't want their parents to think badly of them.

Another reason to remain calm is that even though your child may want you to *listen* to her litanies about why the world is unfair, it doesn't mean she wants you to go out and fight her battles for her. At this age, it doesn't make a child look good (to her peers) to have Mommy or Daddy marching in to make everyone else behave.

How to Help

It is important to be there for your child, though, and to listen when his heart is aching. Try to remember that what seems trivial to you (*another* fight with a best friend, a silly name someone called him) may feel to your child (at least for the moment) like the worst thing that could ever happen to anyone, anywhere.

If your child mentions a conflict or problem, don't dismiss it with a remark like "Oh, he didn't really mean it" or "You don't need him as a friend anymore." Try to draw out more information by asking open-ended questions like: "How did that make you feel?"; "Why do you think he said that?"; "Do you think you could have done anything differently to avoid what happened?"

Once you understand the nature of the problem, share similar experiences from your own past ("I remember how awful I felt in fifth grade when my best friend decided he didn't like me anymore and became friends with another kid..."). Let your child know that these kinds of experiences are common at this age, and that he has the inner strength to get through the crisis, just as you did.

Be careful about giving too much direct advice, though (as in: "You should call your friend right now and tell him ..."). Fifth graders prefer to puzzle out their own solutions. Help him brainstorm ("Can you think of anything you could do to resolve this situation? What if you tried doing this...?"). Then, let him attempt to resolve whatever conflict there is on his own.

The Next Step

If you suspect (or know) that your child is being persistently bullied, threatened, or pressured to engage in unhealthy, unpleasant, or unlawful behavior, and he can't handle it on his own, you should step in—especially if there's any possibility of physical harm. As one teacher notes, "I once had a girl who could barely multiply, but was so up on the latest fashions that half the class hung on her every word. When a shyer girl in the class dared to wear a more fashionable outfit one day, the popular girl threatened to beat her up after school. I'm not sure what would have happened if the parents hadn't told me, so

I could intervene. But nowadays, you can't take any chances."

You should also step in if your child seems to have no friends at all. That, too, can signal an underlying problem. Every child needs at least one friend at this stage. So if your child is being shunned by classmates or is purposely avoiding them you need to find out why.

With a fifth grader, however, you should always ask permission before calling the teacher about peer problems. For example, you could say, "I'm really concerned about this situation and I'd like to talk to the teacher about it because I think she could help. Would that be okay with you?" Otherwise, if you go to the teacher and your child finds out about it secondhand, he might feel that you've betrayed his confidence. And with a preteen—that's a *major* offense. It could mean the end of his desire to tell you anything else he's feeling.

If your child says no, and you still think the problem is pressing enough to bring to the teacher's or principal's attention, explain how you feel and why. Or agree together on another adult associated with the school who might be able to help (his baseball coach, for example, or the school psychologist or nurse).

Coping with Peer Pressure

Many different factors influence the power of peer pressure at this point, such as where you live, what your child is allowed to watch on TV, who her friends are, and what kind of tone the teacher sets in the classroom. But whether it becomes intense this year or remains relatively mild, you shouldn't feel helpless. There is still a

great deal you can do to prevent your child from blindly
following the crowd.

- *Talk about and model your values.* Don't just assume
  your child knows how you feel or what you think. Tell
  her. When you see smoking or violence glamorized in
  movies or TV shows, mention how that makes you
  feel. When there's someone in the news who's done
  something extraordinary for other people, comment
  on how much you admire that behavior. When you see
  a friend or neighbor in need, set an example of caring—and have your child help you. Fifth graders don't
  need long lectures: They need lots of little conversations and good role models.

- *Set limits on trends.* Just because your child complains that every other fifth grade parent in the
  school thinks it's okay for a ten-year-old to pierce her
  nostrils, dye her hair, stay up until eleven P.M. watching television on school nights, or go on dates, it doesn't
  mean your child will be traumatized if you say no. It's
  still your job to set the limits you feel are fair, reasonable, and safe.

    However, you should pick your battles carefully now,
  or your child may start to tune everything out. If you're
  coming down hard on an issue like not doing homework, for example, you may need to back off on something less harmful, like wearing a piece of trendy clothing.

- *Supervise play dates and group activities.* Your child
  isn't going to want you nosing around during play
  dates anymore. But you—or another responsible

adult—should always be within range when fifth
graders are getting together. This is no time for kids-
only parties. Fifth graders may be more mature, but
most of them aren't ready to be left completely unsupervised for any length of time.

- *Use peer pressure to teach good lessons.* For example,
  if everyone in the class is into wearing a sneaker
  brand you feel is outrageously priced, cut a deal with
  your child: Tell him how much you're willing to spend
  on his sneakers and let him earn the difference for the
  sneakers he wants by doing extra work around the
  house.

- *Get your child involved in after-school pursuits.* "What
  really helped my daughter in fifth grade was getting
  involved in horseback riding, something she had
  dreamed about doing for years," notes Beth Gillespie.
  "Kids who aren't part of the popular crowd at this
  stage need an outside activity," she adds. "Just knowing you have something to look forward to that makes
  you feel fulfilled makes it easier to resist the pressure
  to follow the crowd."

The After-School Schedule

Your biggest problem will probably be overscheduling.
Fifth graders have lots of interests and enthusiasm and a
very high desire to be with friends. But they still aren't
very good at setting priorities. They need—and want—
parental help. In addition, most fifth graders need at least
two free afternoons a week, so they can get their homework
done.

You should also be regulating TV time. Among other things, it can hamper studying and discourage physical activity. And there are a lot of programs aired during prime time that aren't exactly appropriate for ten-year-olds.

Keep in mind, too, that along with the usual fare—music lessons, religious groups, and sports—kids this age are often interested in helping others. In particular, many fifth graders love to work with younger kids, as well as with senior citizens. So this is a good time to get them involved with community service activities.

Save Time for You

While you should encourage activities and friendships, you shouldn't let them take over your child's life. Fifth graders still need family time. The problem is, they don't actively want it anymore. So you may have to be a little more creative to get your child's attention. Here are some strategies that'll help:

- *Designate a block of time as "family time" once a week,* and make it clear that—like it or not—you all have to do something fun together. It could be anything from going to the movies or on a picnic to making popcorn and watching a video, playing whiffle ball in the back yard, or playing board games all afternoon. Put on the answering machine, turn off the television, put away your work—and try to enjoy just being a family.

- *Find out what your child loves most about what she's studying in (or after) school*—and then plan an outing to a museum, a historic site, or another set-

ting to reinforce it. A Civil War buff might enjoy visiting a local battlefield, for instance; a budding bal-
lerina or Broadway singer might enjoy a night out
at the ballet or the theater; a baseball nut would
probably love to see the game live, in a real baseball
stadium—even if it means sitting next to Mom or
Dad.

- *Ask your child for help with preparing meals or baking.* Or do something else together that benefits the
  whole family.

- *Let your child plan an afternoon out with you.* Tell
  him you are willing to do anything he wants that's
  safe, reasonable, and affordable.

- *Invite your child to contribute ideas to make
  traditional family get-togethers (at Thanksgiving,
  for instance) more meaningful and enjoyable for her.*

- *Stop what you're doing now and then to just sit and
  listen (without critiquing)* as your child practices a
  music lesson; cheer him on from the sidelines during
  a sports practice; be her audience when she's preparing for a play or an oral report at school.

- *Take turns reading chapters to each other from a book
  you both love.*

Above all, try to keep these special times together
positive. Don't use them as opportunities to "teach
your child a lesson" or "help her improve." Just enjoy
each other. The memories you create now will help

both of you survive the tension of the teenage years ahead.

Looking Ahead

Moving on to sixth grade is a big step for many children, especially if it involves attending a new school. There will be new people to meet, new teachers to please, new friendships to form, and a new environment to figure out. Your child will also be changing classrooms and teachers more frequently and doing more independent learning through homework.

Even if your child isn't switching schools, there may be more pressure for her to act grown-up. Plus, after school, her social life will be heating up, and she may be moving into more competitive situations with her sports, lessons, and other after-school activities. There may be more tension at home, too, as adolescent attitudes and behaviors kick in.

It's a lot for an eleven- or twelve-year-old to handle. So don't be surprised if your child has mixed feelings about the changes ahead. As Janet Schwartz notes, "I can tell my son is ready to move beyond elementary school because he keeps complaining now that 'They treat us like babies at school!' But he's also somewhat terrified about making the transition to middle school. There are so many questions and unknowns for him. It's going to be a big jump."

The same strategies you used in preparing your child for kindergarten will help now, too. Be positive about the new school. Be supportive when your child voices concerns or asks questions. Find a chance for him to visit the school. And have him talk to other children who have gone there.

Most of all, don't forget that your child is still a child. He may not want you to kiss him in broad daylight anymore, but he still wants—and needs—your attention, as well as an occasional hug.

Chapter 7:

All Grades

The Ten Best Ways to Help Your Child Succeed in School

When I asked teachers in grades K–5 what they thought parents should do to ensure success in school, I was surprised to hear the same bits of advice over and over again. Here's what teachers at every grade level wish more parents would do—more often:

1. ENCOURAGE READING IN ANY WAY YOU CAN

There is no way to overestimate the importance of reading. It not only enhances learning in all of the other subject areas, it exposes children to a wealth of information and experiences they might not otherwise enjoy. It stimulates the imagination, nourishes emotional growth, builds verbal skills, and influences analyzing and thinking. In fact, according to every teacher I interviewed, reading *to* or *with* your child every day is the single most important thing you can do—at every grade level, from kindergarten through fifth.

But you shouldn't worry so much about *how well* your child is reading in any particular grade. Different children acquire reading skills at different ages and in different ways. And you can't force a child who's not ready to start reading.

But you can promote a love of reading by giving your child lots of fun experiences with print at whatever level she's in. Here are some reading milestones you should look for (with the *approximate* grades when they first appear), and specific tips on how to help.

FROM PRESCHOOL THROUGH KINDERGARTEN

MILESTONE #1: Your child enjoys looking at books and being read to but doesn't realize that the print—not the pictures or the reader—tells the story.

How to Help

- Have your child dictate stories or letters to you. Write them down exactly as he says them and read them back to him, pointing to the words as you read.
- Read lots of short, simple books aloud, including alphabet books.
- Reread your child's favorite books as often as she asks (even if it starts to drive you crazy).
- Leave magnetic letters on the refrigerator for your child to fool around with.
- Talk about the sounds different letters make.
- Give alphabet puzzles, alphabet blocks, and books to your child for birthday gifts and other special occasions.

- Make an audiotape of yourself reading your child's favorite book so she can listen to it while looking at the book when you're not around.

  MILESTONE #2: Your child pretends to read simple, repetitive books using his memory.

How to Help

- Point to words as you read books, lists, labels, cards, signs, and even cereal boxes to your child.
- Let him finish a familiar sentence in a book or say a word that's frequently repeated in a story every time you point to it (as in "Go, Dog. *Go*" or "Green Eggs and Ham").
- Tape word labels (such as "door," "chair," or "bed") on different objects around the house or in your child's room.
- Teach your child to read her first name by writing it for her, labeling her belongings, and having her outline the letters (for a sign in her room) with beans, beads, crayons, or other art materials.

FROM KINDERGARTEN THROUGH FIRST GRADE

  MILESTONE #3: Your child realizes that individual printed words represent individual spoken words and begins to recognize and read a few— such as dog, car, and no, plus his own name.

How to Help

- Read together every day.
- Encourage your child to point to words as he "reads" a book.

- Help her learn to write and identify uppercase and lowercase letters.
- Teach him how to spell and write familiar words and names.
- Play word-related games (as in: "I'm going to eat something on this table that begins with the letter *B*. Can you guess what it is?" or "Let's say all the words we can think of that start with the letter *T*").
- Together, come up with a list of short, simple words that rhyme (such as *bat, cat, sat, rat, hat*). Write them down in a column, so your child can see how part of each word is similar.

> *MILESTONE #4: Your child can read simple, repetitive books using the text or illustrations to figure out unfamiliar words.*

How to Help

- Read a new book aloud several times before encouraging your child to tackle it on his own.
- Listen to your child read and help—if asked—with problem words. Act like it's no big deal if he misses some. Concentrate, instead, on making the experience fun.
- If your child misses a lot of words while reading and starts acting frustrated, offer to take over the reading or choose an easier book. Never force your child to read a book that's too hard just because his friends can read it or his sister could when she was his age.
- Help your child write and read his own stories and books. Accept whatever spellings she uses, even if it's only the initial letters of each word.
- Get your child her own library card.

FROM FIRST GRADE THROUGH THIRD

MILESTONE #5: Your child begins to read short illustrated books on her own, for enjoyment.

How to Help

- Make frequent trips to the local library and encourage your child to pick out her own books.
- Let your child select at least one book from the school book order form each month. (This has a double benefit, since the more books children order, the more free books the teacher can get for use by all of the students in the classroom.)
- When your child is reading to you, casually supply the words she doesn't know or can't figure out. Encouragement is still more important than correction.
- Play games that involve reading skills (for example, have a treasure hunt and place written clues around the house; play Junior Scrabble and other age-appropriate board games).
- Ask your child to read to a younger friend or sibling.
- Leave your child brief notes—to say "I love you" or "Good luck" or "Don't forget to take your homework to school"—in her lunch box, near her cereal bowl at breakfast, or on the bathroom mirror.
- Give books as gifts.
- Limit TV, computer, and Nintendo time, and encourage your child to read instead—even if it's only his baseball cards or some comic books.

MILESTONE #6: Your child begins to read longer books with fewer illustrations and distinct chapters (chapter books).

How to Help

- Take turns reading the pages aloud together.
- Talk about the plot, characters, and conflicts in the story you're reading together.
- Explain complex words and sentences; help with pronunciations.
- Encourage your child to read you recipes and other written directions.
- Show how much you value reading by doing a lot of it yourself. Ask for books when it's your turn to get gifts.
- Talk about the books or magazine articles you're reading and enjoying.

FROM THIRD GRADE THROUGH FIFTH

MILESTONE #7: Your child can read independently and enjoys reading a variety of books.

How to Help

- Make sure there are lots of different kinds of reading materials geared to his interests around the house (for instance, a kid-oriented sports magazine or books on the sports or other activities your child loves).
- Treat your child like a reading expert, no matter what kinds of books she loves to read. If she's a horror story addict, for instance, say: "You've been reading a lot of those horror story books. Which one do you think is best? Why?"
- Make sure your child has some free time every day when he can curl up in a chair and read. Read your own books, magazines, or newspapers when your child is reading.

- Keep reading aloud to your child (to strengthen his vocabulary, comprehension, and listening skills, as well as his enjoyment of reading).

---

2. TREAT YOUR CHILD AS THOUGH HE'S AN AUTHOR

He doesn't have to be Hemingway or Shakespeare. All he has to do is grow up thinking that he can put thoughts and words onto paper. And the sooner he starts, the better.

As with reading, you can help in different ways at different stages of development. Look for these milestones (at these *approximate* grade levels), and use these tips.

FROM PRESCHOOL THROUGH FIRST GRADE

MILESTONE #1: Your child can scribble or draw a picture and associate words with the picture (such as, "This is the sun" or "This is me").

How to Help

- Provide lots of materials (paper, markers, crayons, paints, chalk) and time for drawing.
- Ask your child to tell you about the pictures she draws and label the objects as she points them out.
- Ask your child to dictate stories or poems to go with the pictures he draws and write them down for him. Then, read his work aloud, exactly as he dictated it.

MILESTONE #2: Your child begins to produce marks on a page that resemble written words and can "read" you what he's written.

How to Help

- Encourage your child to "read" you his words, and express your enjoyment ("What a wonderful story!" or "Thank you so much for sharing that with me").
- Keep providing the materials and time for your child to write her own stories and books.
- Write stories and poems alongside your child and read to her what you've written (even if you think it's awful—your child won't judge it).

MILESTONE #3: Your child understands that sounds are represented by certain letters and begins to write actual letters to represent real words ("sn" for sun, *for instance).*

How to Help

- Encourage your child to write notes, keep a journal, or write her own books.
- Offer to rewrite his words or sentences using the real spellings.
- When you're reading together, point out how most sentences have the first letter of the first word capitalized, spaces between each separate word, and a period at the end.
- Mention who the author is when you read books together, and talk about what authors (and illustrators) do. Point out that when your child writes stories, he's an author, too.

FROM FIRST GRADE THROUGH SECOND

MILESTONE #4: Your child begins to fill out the words she writes, using more standardized spellings.

How to Help

- Don't act overly concerned about spelling. Instead, continue to praise your child for the imagination and ideas he expresses in writing.
- Gently correct spelling on school homework assignments (when the teacher requests it). Your attitude should convey "Let me help you" rather than "Get it right!"
- Reinforce the idea that a piece of written work rarely just happens: It gets written, edited, proofread, and rewritten before the final copy is published.
- Let your child create a quiet writing corner in the house, and encourage her to write frequently. Give her ideas about what to write if she's stumped. For instance: "Write a note to Grandma to say thank you for the birthday present," "Write down your favorite memory from when you were little," or "Write a story about your favorite toy."
- Have your child write lists—of anything from what she wants for her birthday or what her favorite movies are to what she loves most about school or what she wants you to buy at the grocery store for snacks.
- Let your child see you writing, and talk about how you're using writing: to express thanks, for instance, or to communicate information to office mates, lodge a complaint; request vacation information, remember errands, create a shopping list, and so on.

- Get the whole family involved in keeping a vacation or "special days" journal.

FROM THIRD GRADE THROUGH FIFTH

MILESTONE #5: Your child becomes a confident writer and isn't afraid to use improper spellings on her first drafts. She knows she can go back and correct spelling mistakes during the revise stage.

How to Help

- Let your child see you write—and correct your own mistakes; ask him his opinion on something you've written ("Is this note to the teacher clear?").
- Give gifts associated with writing, such as special pencils and pens, a desk lamp, a hardbound diary, a children's dictionary, or personalized stationery.
- Encourage your child to write using the computer; teach her how to use the spell checker.
- Show pride in what your child writes by displaying her books and stories for visitors and other family members to enjoy, or by having her read them aloud.
- Encourage your child to have a pen pal.
- Invite your child to do crossword puzzles, anagrams, and other word games that build vocabulary and fluency.
- Read together, and talk about the books and authors you both love.

3. *MAKE MATH PART OF HER EVERYDAY LIFE*

Leave the flash cards, workbooks, and other skill-and-drill stuff to the teacher. At home, the best way to help your child learn to love math is to play with numbers and to frequently point out the various ways in which math makes our lives easier. By working with tangible objects and counting, sorting, estimating, measuring, looking for patterns, and solving real-life problems, children learn to think in mathematical terms, without worrying whether or not they're "smart enough" to do math.

Almost anything you do that involves numbers and/or problem solving will build your child's math skills. Here are just a few ideas to get you started.

FROM KINDERGARTEN THROUGH SECOND GRADE

- Have your child set the table (counting and sorting the sets of plates, napkins, cups, and silverware).
- Post a running countdown of the days until her birthday. Let her change the number each day.
- Challenge him to guess at things, and then find the answers. For example: "How many bowls of cereal do you think we can get out of this box?"; "How many M&Ms do you think are in your (snack-size) bag? How many red ones? Blue ones?"; "How many minutes do you think it will take to clear off the table?"; "How many licks do you think it will take before you finish that juice pop?"; "Which of these cups do you think will hold more juice?"
- Play a copycat game, where one person creates a pattern (pat your head, touch your knee, clap three times) and the other person has to repeat the pattern three times in a row.
- Ask your child to help you create a pattern for a quilt square or an abstract picture using: markers and paper, construction paper in different colors cut into

square, triangle, and other shapes; or shapes cut out of different fabrics.

- Ask your child to measure things in nontraditional units. For example: "Let's see how many footsteps it takes to get from here to the door. Why do you think it's more for you and fewer for me?"; "How many action figures (or Barbie dolls) long is this table?"

- Have your child compare things: "Which do you think is heavier—a cookie or ten chocolate chips?"; "Who do you think is taller, Mom or Dad?"; "Which carrot is longer? Fatter? Crunchier?"

- Give your child problems to solve—and let her work them out by touching and counting actual objects. For example: "I have four cookies here, but two people want to eat them. How many should each person get?"; "If we invite six kids to your birthday party and put two candy bars in each kid's treat bag, how many candy bars will we use?"

FROM THIRD GRADE THROUGH FIFTH

All of the above, plus:

- Play board games, dice games, and card games (such as War) with your child. Encourage her to make up her own games.

- Talk about how you use math when you're balancing your checkbook, paying cashiers, changing bills for coins or vice versa, setting your household budget, depositing money in the bank, buying birthday gifts, and so on.

- Teach your child to budget his own money—by helping him save up for a special toy or activity.

- Involve your child in measuring ingredients for recipes.
- Ask for help with food shopping ("Which is the better deal here?"; "How much does each one cost per pound?"; "Which cereal has more grams of sugar?"; "If they cost fifty cents apiece, how much will it be if I buy three?"). Let him bring his calculator to the grocery store.
- Encourage your child to think of different solutions to problems. For example: "You have twenty dollars of birthday money to spend. Try to come up with three different ways to spend it"; "What are some different ways we could help ourselves remember to bring back these library books within two weeks?"; "We lost one of the dice for this game. What else could we use to figure out how many spaces to move our players?"

Most of all, try to be positive about math—even if it was your worst subject in school. If your child's having trouble in it or starts complaining that it's too hard or too boring, act as though you know that if she keeps on trying, she'll improve. "Everyone learns at different rates and in different ways," you could say. "That's why we have teachers. But I know you can do it if you keep on trying."

4. TEACH YOUR CHILD HOW TO LISTEN

Teachers who've been around for fifteen or more years say they've seen a definite decline in childrens' attention spans and listening skills since they first started teaching. Many of them attribute this not only to the fast and entertaining pace of television and computer games, but to the fact that many children today don't have a lot of time to just sit around, listening and talking to family members. Between parents' jobs and childrens' after-school activities, it's hard, sometimes, to get everyone in the same room for a family dinner once a week.

But being able to focus on what other people are saying is an important element in learning. So, whenever possible, try to build your child's listening skills. Here are some strategies that will help.

- Read aloud to your child on a regular basis—even after she has learned to read by herself. Ask questions as you read, to make sure your child is understanding what she hears.
- Limit television, computer, and Nintendo time. While they're all entertaining and can even be educational, they tend to promote tunnel vision. Make sure the time your child spends in front of a screen is balanced by time spent with other people, talking face-to-face.
- When you speak to your child, make eye contact and gently touch his shoulder or arm to secure his attention.
- When giving directions, ask your child to repeat back to you what she heard you say—to make sure she really did hear and does understand what she needs to do.
- Model good listening behaviors. When your child wants to talk to you, for example, stop what you're doing and look at him while he's speaking. When he's finished, say something that indicates you heard him, even if you only repeat back what he said: "So, you want to stay up a little later tonight to watch the All-Star game."
- Play talking and listening games with your child, like Charades, Red Light/Green Light, Duck, Duck,

Goose, and Twenty Questions.

- Teach your child that even if an adult is saying something he finds boring, he still needs to listen, look at the person, and show respect.

- Spend time with your child doing quiet activities that encourage conversation, such as taking a walk together, taking a ride in the car, folding laundry, or picking strawberries.

---

5. SUPPORT YOUR CHILD'S TEACHER AND THE SCHOOL RULES

Even if you don't agree with them. It doesn't do any child any good to hear her parents say that school is "a waste of time," that school rules are "dumb," or that what she's learning is "stupid" or "useless." Your child doesn't have a choice about going to school, so she might as well feel good about where she's spending her time. She'll be more motivated to work hard and succeed if she thinks *you* think that what she's doing is worthwhile.

So even if a school rule seems silly or unfair to you, or you think your child's teacher is dead wrong about something, don't make a big issue about it *in front of your child*. Instead, take your concerns straight to the source.

THE KEY STEPS TOWARD RESOLUTION

The best way to approach a problem or disagreement involving the school is to:

- *Make an appointment to see or speak to the teacher.* For minor problems and concerns, a telephone conference might be sufficient. But if you feel the issue merits more serious discussion, arrange to meet with the teacher face-to-face. Don't try to corner her before or after school, when her focus is on the students. Instead, schedule a time when she can give you her full attention.

- *Consider carefully what you want to say before you visit the school.* Write down a list of your concerns and why they're concerns. Let your list rest for a while and then go back to it when you're feeling calm and rational. Try to frame all of your concerns in the most positive light possible, so you won't immediately put the teacher on the defensive. For example, instead of saying, "You're not doing anything to help my child improve in reading," you should say "I'm really concerned about my child's progress in reading. I wanted to check in with you to see if there's anything else that can be done, at school and at home, to help her move forward."

  If necessary, practice your spiel in front of a third party, to make sure you don't sound too threatening. You may feel like blasting the teacher; you may even have good reason to do so. But your child will not benefit in any way if you alienate her teacher. Try to remember that the best school solutions come when teacher and parent act as a team.

- *When you meet with the teacher, voice your concerns in the least threatening, most friendly tone you can muster.* If you lose your temper, you may lose the chance to be taken seriously. Remind yourself that your goal is to help your child, not blow off steam. If possible, bring tangible evidence to back up your side of the story.

- *Prepare to listen to the teacher's side.* There may be mitigating factors that you're unaware of, you may have gotten the wrong information from your child; or there may be a miscommunication that's complicating the issue. Try to be—and act—open-minded.

- *If you and the teacher cannot come to a mutually satisfying solution, enlist the principal (or the school's psychologist or a learning specialist).* "I appreciate what you're saying, but I'm still concerned," you might say. "I'd feel more comfortable if I got another opinion on the matter. I'd like to meet with the principal." Or, if you're afraid the teacher will take her anger at you out on your child (this shouldn't happen, but it could), request a private meeting with the principal. If the second meeting doesn't help, the next step is to contact the superintendent. But only you can decide whether or not that's necessary.

Sometimes you just have to accept a less-than-perfect teacher or classroom situation. In most cases, it won't do permanent damage to your child—and it might even help him develop some healthy coping skills. Also, sometimes things that upset parents about school don't really bother the students. So you might want to talk to your child first, before forging ahead with a complaint or requesting a transfer for your child. In some cases, moving a child from one classroom to another midyear would be worse— from the child's point of view—than having him stick it out with a weak teacher.

On the other hand, *you shouldn't feel intimidated by school personnel.* If you feel you have a legitimate complaint (or if your child's health, safety, or welfare is at stake) and your gut keeps telling you to fight for your child, you should do that. Just try to remember at every step of the way that the less hostility you communicate, the more likely people will be to listen carefully to your concerns and work toward a mutually acceptable solution. Let the power of persistence—rather than the impact of aggression—carry your case.

IF THE TEACHER CALLS YOU

The steps outlined above should also be followed if the teacher calls *you* to discuss problems your child is causing at school. Even if you think the teacher is wrong, or your child insists that she's innocent, go into the conference with your mind open and your demeanor calm and friendly. Most teachers aren't "out to get" their students; they genuinely want to make every child's school year a success.

---

6. TELL THE TEACHER EVERYTHING

That is, everything that's happening at home that might affect how your child behaves in school. That includes positive changes (such as the birth of a baby; a move to a bigger and better house; an invitation for your child to compete in a gymnastics or violin competition, or a vacation to Disney World), as well as negative ones (a separation or divorce, a death or illness in the family, a parent who's lost a job).

It's not that teachers are nosy. It's that most children are not terribly skilled at handling excitement or coping with changes or stress. And they all carry their baggage from home into the classroom. Even something little, like a fight with a sibling in the car on the way to school, can affect a child's behavior or performance at school.

If a teacher knows there's a problem or change at home, she's less likely to react inappropriately when behavior goes awry at school. Under normal circumstances, for instance, a dip in grades might prompt a teacher to suggest extra help or tutoring. If she knows that the child just got a new baby sister, however, she might react instead by pulling the child aside and inviting her to talk about how she's feeling now that she's a big sister.

You needn't go into all of the gory details of what's happening at home, either. All the teacher expects to hear is "I just wanted to let you know that we're moving to a new house next week, and Allan is pretty nervous about the whole thing" or "If Sheila seems a little hyper these days it's because her aunt is taking her to her first Broadway play this weekend."

What else do teachers want to know?

- *How your child feels about school.* Is she unhappy? Does she think it's too hard? Is she complaining about it at home? Or does she like it? Is there some special activity that she really enjoyed? Does she talk about the things she learns in school?

  Most teachers would rather hear about problems sooner than later, so they can work on turning things around as quickly as possible. They—like the rest of us—also appreciate a kind or encouraging word now and then. So don't forget to mention the good stuff.

- *How your child feels about school friends.* Is she making any? Does she feel like a part of the class—or an outcast? Is she being teased or harassed? Is she too shy to make new friends? Does she need to branch out from her one best friend and get to know other kids?

In elementary school, there is still a lot teachers can do to mold social relationships. But they need to know what the problem is before they can start to solve it.

- *What your child's special passions are.* Sometimes, a child who is a reluctant reader can be drawn to books that speak to a special interest, such as sports or pirates or ice skating or animals. Or, a desire to write might be stimulated by an invitation to describe one of the subjects your child loves. Let the teacher know if there is something that really motivates your child, so she can capitalize on it in the classroom.

- *What your child's special needs are.* That includes any-thing from allergies to phobias, physical or medical conditions, learning problems or preferences, special talents, emotional concerns, and behavioral patterns. If you think an issue might come up in these or other areas, let the teacher know.

---

7. MAKE SURE YOUR CHILD IS READY FOR SCHOOL

All through elementary school, it's the parent's job to make sure a child:

- *Gets to bed at a reasonable hour.* That means around seven-thirty to eight P.M. for younger children, and eight-thirty to nine P.M. for fourth and fifth graders.

Children who regularly go to bed later on school nights have a hard time keeping up in school, teachers say. They end up being tired and grouchy, they're more likely to have behavioral problems, and they aren't able to fulfill their academic potential. Even sleep specialists are now beginning to believe that certain behavioral and learning problems among children are the result of undetected sleep deprivation.

The bottom line is that a good night's sleep is the best guarantee of a pleasant and productive day at school.

- *Eats a filling and nutritious breakfast.* Children who skip breakfast might not feel hungry when they first get to school, but according to teachers, they usually hit a slump around mid-morning and can't keep their minds on schoolwork until sometime after lunch.

   If your child doesn't like the traditional foods kids eat for breakfast—cereal, milk, juice, and toast—let him eat what he does like. There's nothing nutritionally wrong with eating pizza or a peanut butter sandwich in the morning. Or, if all else fails, send him to school with a breakfast bar and a box of juice, so he can get *something* in his belly before the first bell rings.

- *Wears the proper clothes for both the day's activities and the weather.* A kid who goes to school without mittens, a hat, or boots in the winter might have to sit inside for recess while her classmates spend their excess energy on the playground. A child who doesn't have shorts and sneakers on gym day might end up sitting on the sidelines while everyone else is running around having fun.

Children don't always have the best judgment when it comes to protective clothing. (If it's warm in the house, they assume it's going to be warm outside, for example.) And they don't always remember which days they have gym or other special activities. So it's up to you to tell your child what to expect in terms of weather, and what to wear—or at least *bring*—to school.

- *Labels all belongings.* That includes his backpack, lunch box, books, school supplies, gym clothes, gym bag, art smock—and any other piece of clothing or personal item that might somehow get separated from him during the school day. Even ten-year-olds aren't that reliable when it comes to identifying their own clothing from a heap on the locker room floor.

- *Has a lunch or lunch money.* Most children aren't thinking about lunch when they run out to meet the bus or jump in the car in the morning. It's your job to either make it, take it, or remind your child to remember lunch.

- *Puts her homework in her backpack to bring to school.* Fourth or fifth graders may be able to do this on their own, but it never hurts to ask "Got your homework?" before your child slips out the door.

- *Remembers to bring special supplies for special days.* There's nothing more devastating to a young child than to be the only kid who forgot his teddy bear on the day the class was having a teddy bear picnic at school. Or to show up on picture day wearing his rattiest clothes. Or to forget to wear the class colors for the all-school field day. These are the kinds of details most kids (and parents) have a hard time remembering. So it's your job to find a way to help you both stay on top of teacher requests. Hang up a big calendar with important dates circled in red, for instance, or put up Post-it notes on the bathroom mirror the night before a special day at school.

- *Knows exactly who will pick her up and what will happen when the school day ends.* Children will worry all day long if they don't know what to expect when that final bell rings. So remind your child when she's leaving home: "I'll see you at the corner when the bus drops you off at three P.M." or "I'll be home from work at six P.M.. Then we'll have supper and I'll check your homework." If you anticipate *any* change in the daily routine, or in the person greeting your child after school, make sure you give plenty of notice.

- *Gets to school on time—every day.* Chronic lateness is not only disruptive to the entire class, it can make a child feel out-of-step all day. Plus, it sends a message that school is not important enough to be on time for.

8. *SPEND TIME IN YOUR CHILD'S CLASSROOM*

Even if it's only once a year, and you have to take a half day off from work to do it. All children, even the "too cool for school" fifth graders, get a real thrill when they see their parents in their classroom. It sends a powerful message that you care about your child and about her education.

Seeing the classroom firsthand is also the best way for

you to get a perspective on what and how the teacher is teaching, what kinds of challenges the teacher is facing, what the class chemistry is, how your child fits in within the group, and how she interacts with specific peers. Plus, it will give you a better idea of the kinds of questions you should ask to draw your child out when talking about school (see tip 10).

In most schools, you don't need an excuse to visit the classroom. Just ask the teacher if you can come in and observe. If you want an excuse, volunteer. Teachers are always looking for parents to help with everything from handling class book orders to:

- sharing expertise in a particular subject area related to your job or hobbies
- reading to children
- conducting writing workshops or helping children "publish" their books
- tutoring kids who need extra help or working with a small group of advanced students in math or other subjects
- chaperoning field trips
- sewing costumes for a school play, baking cupcakes for a party, or cutting out paper shapes for a class project
- typing up a classroom newsletter or literary magazine.

If you have lots of time to give, you might consider:

- being a "class parent" (the person who acts as a liaison between the teacher and the other parents—

rounding up chaperones for school trips, for in
or finding volunteers to bake for the class bake sales)
- being a playground monitor
- joining the school's parent/teacher association
- joining the principal's school advisory committee (if
  there is one)
- running for your local school board.

At the very least, you should plan to make time in
your busy schedule to attend:

- special events to which parents are invited (a
  Mother's Day Brunch prepared by the children, for
  instance, or a Writer's Tea, at which children read
  their stories aloud to their parents)
- special school events, such as the annual holiday
  show or spring musical
- the school's annual open house
- all of the scheduled parent/teacher conferences.

---

9. ENCOURAGE RESPONSIBILITY
AND INDEPENDENCE

Both of these are essential to independent learning. And
both will make it easier for your child to adjust to the
demands of school and get along with his teacher and
classmates. So, whenever possible, let your child do
things for himself—and for others.

For example, encourage him to:

- *Play an active role in getting ready for school.* That
  includes picking out school clothes (preferably the
  night before), getting up on time (using an alarm

clock, if necessary), getting dressed, washing up and brushing his teeth, getting his own breakfast ready, making up his bed, and checking to make sure he has everything he needs in his backpack. Younger children will need help, of course. But once your child is physically capable of doing these things, let him take charge. If necessary, make a checklist to help him remember everything that needs to be done.

- *Develop a homework routine.* While there's no set formula, it will help if your child has a regular time and place to do her homework each day. That way she's less likely to forget to do it, and less likely to fight about doing it "later on."

- *Unpack his own backpack.* Teach him that as soon as he gets home from school he should unpack his backpack, put his homework materials in his homework place, and hand you (or put in a special place) any newsletters, notes from the teacher, papers to sign, or special work he's brought home. *Then* he can watch TV, or have his snack, or do whatever else is planned.

  If you make this part of a daily routine, you're less likely to be hit during the morning rush with "Oh no! I'm supposed to bring in cupcakes for the party today" or "Today's the day you're supposed to come to school for our science fair."

- *Pick up her own mess.* That includes toys scattered on the living room floor, clothes left in heaps around the bedroom, bikes and roller skates left out on the driveway, empty CD and video boxes scattered around the family room, snack plates sprinkled with crumbs on the dining room table, and wet towels left cold and lonely on the bathroom floor. It might take longer and require more effort for you to insist that your child pick things up herself, but in the long run it's better for her than having you always do it. In school, she won't have a choice.

- *Get involved in family meals.* Younger children can set the table or help with the grocery list; older kids can often fix their own breakfast, make their own lunch, and help plan meals and shop for food.

- *Perform regular chores that benefit the entire family.* Even little things like taking out the trash regularly or mowing the lawn will help your child see herself as part of a larger family team. They'll also build her sense of competence and confidence.

- *Be accountable for his actions.* If the teacher calls up and says she caught your child cheating, she hasn't seen homework from your child in two weeks, or your child hasn't passed in a major project yet, don't jump to your child's defense with excuses. Instead, schedule a meeting with your child and the teacher to find out why he's slacking off or misbehaving, and establish a mutually satisfactory consequence. Make it clear that your child has to take responsibility for his own actions, even if it means getting a poor grade or being grounded.

10. ASK YOUR CHILD ABOUT SCHOOL EVERY DAY

It isn't always easy to get the scoop on school from your own child. If you ask a perfectly normal, sincere question like "What did you do at school today?" you're likely to get the classic response: "Nothing."

One reason is that so many things happen in the classroom that it's hard for the average child to answer a question like that. She can't remember everything she did, and even if she could, she wouldn't know where to start. It doesn't help to ask "What did you learn at school today?" or "How was school today?" either. Both will elicit one-word answers ("Nothing" or "Fine"), because they're too broad and too vague for most children to process.

But it's still important to ask about school because it teaches your child that school is important and that you really are interested in her life. So how can you get your child to open up? Here's what other parents say really works:

- *Don't ask too soon.* "When my son Max gets off the bus, the last thing he wants to do is talk about school," says Mary Mitchell. "He's too busy thinking about playing with his toys or visiting his friends. So I've learned to let him chill out and play awhile before asking any questions."

- *Develop a ritual.* "For some reason, the only time my five-year-old son, Jack, really opens up about school is when he's taking a bath," says Tamara Eberlein. "So every night, when he gets into the tub, my husband sits with him for ten or fifteen minutes and Jack tells him everything that happened at school. He really looks forward to that time with his father."

"For my son, the magic moment is bedtime," says Charles James. "He's probably just trying to stall me, so he can stay up later. But when he's all tucked in and the lights are off, I hear the most detailed descriptions about school."

- *Ask specific questions.* "I get the best responses when I ask my son about something I'm pretty sure he did at school that day," says Julie Ritzer Ross. For instance: "Did the teacher read any new books today? Did you learn any new songs during music class? Who sat next to you at lunch? How did you do on your spelling test?" The more specific you can be, the better.

- *Read everything the teacher sends home.* "The notes and newsletters that come home in my son's backpack are really the most reliable sources of information," says Charles James. "I find out what my son is learning about, what's coming up in terms of special events or field trips, what kind of help the teacher could use in the classroom, and what I can do at home to reinforce what my son is learning in school. It's not always easy to find time to read them, but it's worth the effort because it helps me fill in the blanks from conversations with my son."

- *Give your child space.* Some children like to think of school as their own private world, where their parents and siblings can't intrude. If your child is like that, don't push. Let him know you're interested in his school day, and let him approach you if he has anything really important to share. Then stay in touch behind the scenes with the teacher, to make sure everything's going okay.

W*hat should I do if my child is academically ahead of
her classmates?*

There is no easy answer to this question. Since most elementary school classrooms include students with a wide
range of academic abilities, there's always a danger that
the children who are working above grade level will
either become bored and misbehave or won't receive the
kind of stimulation that encourages them to fulfill their
academic potential.

In addition, there are many different kinds of intelligence and different levels and rates of growth. A child
who is academically ahead of his classmates, for
instance, may be emotionally or socially behind. He may
be extremely talented in one subject and only average in
the others. Or, his IQ may be off the charts—and his
behavior may be a chronic problem.

Most teachers will tell you that one of the hardest parts of their job is juggling the strengths and weaknesses of all their students, so that each one can experience progress and growth. However, most do make a special effort to challenge their brightest students. For example, they'll often have them:

- participate in mini-lessons, to learn material they're ready for, but their classmates are not
- work individually or as a small group on special projects (such as creating their own board games, writing and performing a skit based on a historical event, or building a model space station)
- work in a higher level textbook for subjects they're way ahead in (such as math)
- do higher level worksheets or homework assignments
- tutor classmates who are struggling with reading or math (teachers say this helps the brighter child strengthen and communicate his own skills)
- participate in open-ended assignments that have no right or wrong answers and can be taken to whatever academic heights each child is capable of attaining. For example: "Write a book about dinosaurs" or "Form a hypothesis and create a science experiment that would enable you to prove or disprove it."

WHAT GIFTED PROGRAMS OFFER

In addition to these special efforts within the classroom, many schools offer enrichment programs for children who are found to be "gifted and talented." But different schools define "gifted" in different ways. In most cases, to be qualified as gifted, a child must be recommended for testing by a teacher. (However, a parent can also request the testing.)

Depending on the school's approach to gifted students, the evaluation process might include an IQ test; a review of the child's scores on standardized tests; an assessment of the child's creative and academic work; tests that measure creativity and special abilities; and an examination of the child's social skills, emotional state, and behavior.

Once they identify gifted children, different schools handle them in different ways. Among the most common approaches are:

- *Providing enrichment on-site.* This usually involves allowing the student to leave her regular classroom for one period, two or three times a week, to take special classes or participate in special activities within the school with other gifted students.

- *Providing enrichment off-site.* In this approach, a gifted child will spend some time in her regular classroom and some time attending special classes in a nearby school that caters to gifted children.

- *Enrolling the child in a special school.* In some school districts, children who are found to be gifted are transferred to a special school that's devoted to gifted students.

- *Having the child skip a grade.* This might include promoting the child ahead a grade level or moving her ahead for classes in one or two subjects.

Each of these approaches has its advantages and disadvantages. And different schools carry them out in different ways, so it's impossible to generalize about which approach is best for which students. You really need to look at what your child's school has to offer and measure it against where she falls in terms of her test results, personality, social skills, emotional maturity, learning style, and other factors.

THE BOTTOM LINE

No matter what your child's school is doing to enrich the academic experiences of bright or gifted children, you should still plan to play a leading role in your child's education. But that doesn't mean you should go out of your way to buy "enrichment" workbooks, computer programs, flash cards, videos, or other expensive learning materials for your exceptional child. Nor should you overload her with after-school enrichment classes. Instead, strive to create an environment that encourages curiosity, exploration, and self-expression. In particular:

- *Read to your child* and make sure she has access to all sorts of reading materials, including books and magazines devoted to her most passionate interests.

- *Make sure he has time to just sit around*—daydreaming, inventing, building, and creating whatever he wants. Exceptionally bright children have a lot going on in their minds, even when it looks like they're just playing with some simple toys.

- *Expose your child to other people, places, cultures, traditions, and experiences as often as you can*—by reading together, watching educational television programs, visiting museums, going to concerts and plays together, and traveling, for instance.

- *Encourage your child to follow her passions,* even if you don't share them. If your child loves science, for example, let her plant a garden and keep a notebook of how different plants grow; if she's into astronomy, challenge her to design a spaceship using odds and ends in the family scrap pile; if she loves to write, ask her to write and illustrate a book for her younger brother's birthday; if she loves telling jokes, offer to videotape her as she performs her own comedy routine. Even gifted children learn best when they're having fun.

- *Introduce him to other gifted students.* While being in a classroom with lots of different types of kids is important in building traits such as tolerance, respect, and empathy, children also need to be around peers who have similar interests and talents. Look for some after-school programs for gifted children who share your child's passions. Encourage your child to be sociable and to develop his friendships, as well as his talents and intellect. Even geniuses need friends.

FOR MORE INFORMATION ON
GIFTED CHILDREN, CONTACT:

Council for Exceptional Children (CEC)
1920 Association Drive
Reston, VA 20191
(703) 620-3660; (888) 232-7733
www.cec.sped.org

**ERIC Clearinghouse on Disabilities and
   Gifted Education**
1920 Association Drive
Reston, VA 20191
(800) 328-0272
www.ced.sped.org/ericec.htm

How can I tell if my child has a learning disability?

Another tough question—mainly because the term
"learning disability" covers so many different types of
problems and conditions that affect learning in children
with *average or above-average intelligence.* In addition,
different school districts use different criteria to define,
diagnose, and treat learning disabilities. And children
who have learning problems also often have physical,
behavioral, or social problems that can complicate both
diagnosis and treatment.

   In general, however, you or your child's teacher may
suspect a learning disability if:

- your child's performance in reading, writing, or
  math is erratic or is far below that of his classmates,
  and
- despite special help he continues to have trouble with
  more than one of the following:

  - *Getting and staying organized* (managing his time,
    completing assignments, locating belongings, making
    decisions, setting priorities, and putting things in
    order, for instance).
  - *Speaking and writing* (especially when attempting
    to follow directions, pronounce words, learn new

words, retell stories, answer questions, understand
things he reads, or write stories).

▪ *Paying attention and remembering information*
(such as the letters of the alphabet or the multiplication tables, directions for assignments, or words he
studied for a spelling test).

▪ *Sticking with activities and assignments until
they're finished* (especially if she frequently feels frustrated and lashes out, cries, or gives up when faced
with a challenge, or if she acts out in class to avoid
having to do her work).

▪ *Making and keeping friends* (due to poor social judgment, impulsive or aggressive behavior, poor sportsmanship, or an inability to read other children's non-
verbal cues).

▪ *Completing physical tasks* (such as cutting, drawing, handwriting, climbing, and running) due to poor
coordination.

None of these, on its own, is a conclusive sign of a
learning disability. Rather, a combination of these
(and other) symptoms may indicate that further testing is in order.

DIAGNOSING A LEARNING PROBLEM

If a learning disability is suspected, the first step is to
take your child to a pediatrician for a complete physical
examination to rule out medical problems like poor vision
or hearing loss. The next step is to obtain neurological,
psychological, and educational assessments (including
intelligence, personality, brain function, and academic performance tests).

If the tests do not showz a learning disability, you'll want to work with the school to find out why your child is performing below his ability level or why he is having specific behavioral problems.

If a learning disability *is* uncovered, you'll need to see what the school can do to help. Depending on the type and intensity of the problem, your child may be given extra help at school or outside tutoring. Or, the school may recommend that he be placed in a special education class or be transferred to another school that is better suited to meeting his particular learning needs.

Whatever the recommendations are, your support of your child, and your acceptance of his disability, will have a major impact on his future success.

FOR MORE INFORMATION ON LEARNING DISABILITIES, CONTACT:

International Dyslexia Association
8600 LaSalle Road
Chester Building, Suite 382
Baltimore, MD 21286-2044
(410) 296-0232; (800) 222-3123
www.interdys.org

ERIC Clearinghouse on Disabilities and Gifted Education
1920 Association Drive
Reston, VA 20191
(800) 328-0272
www.ced.sped.org/ericed.htm

Learning Disabilities Association of America
4156 Library Road
Pittsburgh, PA 15234
(412) 341-1515
www.ldanatl.org

What should I do if my child refuses to go to school?

The easy answer is: Make her go anyway. The sooner children learn that school is not a negotiable option, the better. But also make the effort to find out *why* she doesn't want to go.

It's not uncommon for children to now and then fight about going to school, or to develop stomachaches, headaches, sore throats, or other illnesses in the morning that mysteriously clear up by mid-afternoon (especially on days when a big test is scheduled!). The usual culprits are:

- *Separation anxiety.* This is more common in younger children, but it can happen to any child during the first few days of school. The prospect of leaving home and trading Mom or Dad's one-on-one attention for the fragmented attention of a new teacher, and the stress of having to meet and settle in with a bunch of new kids can be daunting.
  Separation anxiety can also occur:
  - after a child has had a long absence from school (following a vacation or illness, for example)
  - during or following a move to a new home
  - when a family member is ill
  - when someone in the family (or a close friend) has died
  - when something traumatic that happened is being widely discussed or broadcast on the news (a local

child was kidnapped, for instance, or children were killed in a terrorist attack somewhere else in the world)

- when parents are going through a separation or divorce.

In other words, any stress at home or change in routine can trigger it. Usually, if you're consistent about making your child go to school, while reassuring her that she'll have lots of fun at school and you'll be there to pick her up when it's over, this type of school resistance will fade. But be sure to talk to the teacher and the school psychologist, to get their suggestions. You may be able to spend a little extra time with your child in the classroom in the morning, or wait outside the door until you get a signal from the teacher that everything's okay.

- *Fear of school.* This is typically caused by either academic or social concerns. Your child may be doing poorly in one of his subjects, for example, and be worried sick that he'll be called on by the teacher, say something stupid in class, or flunk an upcoming test. He may have an undiagnosed learning disability that's causing him to feel inferior to his classmates. Or, he may simply be fearful of disappointing you with a bad grade, or of not living up to whatever he perceives as your academic standards.

  Fear of going to school can also arise if your child is being:

  - teased, bullied, excluded, or threatened by classmates or older children on the bus, on the playground, or during school
  - treated harshly or unfairly by a teacher, bus driver, or other school professional

- scared by the way a teacher is disciplining or yelling at other students
- intimidated by the way other students are behaving
- sexually, physically, or verbally abused by an older student or an adult at school.

This is why school fears should be carefully addressed—and the sooner the better. Otherwise, they can develop into more serious problems such as learning or social delays, phobias, or panic attacks.

FINDING OUT WHY

Most children aren't articulate or self-aware enough to just come out and tell you why they don't want to go to school. So you'll have to do some sleuthing. The first step is to talk to your child. Tell her that you're concerned about her reluctance to go to school and you really need to find out why. Then, no matter what she tells you, don't just dismiss it with a comment like "That's silly!" or "Teachers don't do those things!" Take her seriously and support her feelings. For example: "It sounds like you're really worried about Grandma dying while you're at school" or "You're afraid that if Daniel can get away with bullying Joe, he might bully you, too."

Then:

- *Give her whatever facts you can.* For instance: "You're right. Grandma is very sick. But the doctors don't think she's going to die. She just needs to stay in the hospital a little longer, until she's strong enough to take care of herself again."

- *Help him brainstorm (and role-play) solutions.* "If

Daniel does try to bully you, what do you think you could do to stay safe? If that doesn't work, what's the next step?"

- *If necessary, let her know you will intervene* by talking to the teacher or, if that doesn't help, the school psychologist or the principal.

- *If necessary, take him for a medical examination* to rule out a real sickness or signs of abuse.

If none of these strategies help, and the school resistance becomes chronic or more intense, or your child begins to withdraw and show other signs of stress, enlist the aid of the school psychologist. Just forcing your child to go to school without addressing the underlying problems can make the situation much worse.

FOR MORE ON SCHOOL PHOBIA, READ:
- *Monsters Under the Bed and Other Childhood Fears,* by Stephen W. Garber, Ph.D., Marianne Daniels Garber, Ph.D., and Robyn Freedman Spizman
- *Solve Your Child's School-Related Problems,* from the National Association of School Psychologists, edited by Michael Martin, Ph.D., NCSP; and Cynthia Waltman-Greenwood, Ph.D., NCSP

OTHER ORGANIZATIONS AND
ASSOCIATIONS YOU MAY FIND HELPFUL

Family Math Program
EQUALS Program
Lawrence Hall of Science
University of California
Berkeley, CA 94720
(510) 642-1823
www.lhs.berkeley.edu

Family Science Program
Northwest EQUALS
Portland State University
Portland, OR 97207
(800) 547-8887, ext. 3045

International Reading Association
800 Barksdale Road
P.O. Box 8139
Newark, DE 19714
(302) 731-1600; (800) 336-READ
www.reading.org

The MegaSkills® Education Center
Home and School Institute
1500 Massachusetts Avenue, NW
Washington, DC 20005
(202) 466-3633; (800) 634-2872
www.megaskillshsi.org

**National Association for the Education
    of Young Children (NAEYC)**
1509 16th Street, NW
Washington, DC 20036
(202) 232-8777; (800) 424-2460
www.naeyc.org

**National Association of
    School Psychologists (NASP)**
4340 East West Highway, Suite 402
Bethesda, MD 20814
(301) 657-0270
www.naspweb.org

National Center for Fair and Open Testing
342 Broadway
Cambridge, MA 02139
(617) 864-4810
www.fairtest.org

National Council of Teachers of Mathematics
1906 Association Drive
Reston, VA 20191-1593
(703) 620-9840
www.nctm.org

National Education Association
1201 16th Street, NW
Washington, DC 20036
(202) 822-7200

National PTA
330 North Wabash, Suite 2100
Chicago, IL 60611
(312) 670-6782; (800) 307-4782
www.pta.org

**National Information Center for Children and
    Youth with Disabilities (NICHCY)**
P.O. Box 1492
Washington, DC 20013-1492
(800) 695-0285
www.nichcy.org

Bibliography and Recommended Reading

BOOKS

Ames, Louise Bates, Ph.D., and Ilg, Frances L., M.D. *Your Five-Year-Old*. Dell Publishing, New York, 1981.
———. *Your Six-Year-Old*. Dell Publishing, New York, 1981.

Ames, Louise Bates, Ph.D., and Haber, Carol Chase, M.A. *Your Seven-Year-Old*. Dell Publishing, New York, 1980.
———. *Your Eight-Year-Old*. Dell Publishing, New York, 1990.
———. *Your Nine-Year-Old*. Dell Publishing, New York, 1991.

Ames, Louise Bates, Ph.D.; Ilg, Frances L., M.D.; and Baker, Sidney M., M.D. *Your Ten- to Fourteen-Year-Old*. Dell Publishing, New York, 1989.

Bautista, Veltisezar B. *How to Teach Your Child: Things to Know from Kindergarten through Grade 6*. Bookhaus Publishers, Farmington Hills, Michigan, 1992.

Bredekamp, Sue. *Developmentally Appropriate Practice in Early Childhood Programs Serving Children from Birth Through Age 8*, expanded edition. National

Association for the Education of Young Children, Washington, D.C., 1990.

Church, Ellen Booth, and Fraser, Guy N. *Everything You Always Wanted to Know About First Grade But Didn't Know Whom to Ask*. Scholastic, New York, 1996.

Cohen, Dorothy H. *The Learning Child*. Schocken Books, New York, 1988.

Deskin, Gerald, Ph.D., and Steckler, Greg, M.A. *The Parent's Answer Book*. Fairview Press, Minneapolis, 1995.

Franck, Irene, and Brownstone, David. *The Parent's Desk Reference*. Prentice-Hall, New York, 1991.

Garber, Stephen W., Ph.D.; Garber, Marianne Daniels, Ph.D.; and Spizman, Robyn Freedman. *Good Behavior*. St. Martin's Press, New York, 1991.

———. *Monsters Under the Bed and Other Childhood Fears*. Villard Books, New York, 1993.

Goldstein, Robin, and Gallant, Janet. *"Stop Treating Me Like a Kid!"* Penguin Books, New York, 1994.

Harrington, Diane, and Young, Laurette. *School Savvy*. Noonday Press. Farrar, Straus and Giroux, New York, 1993.

Henderson, Anne T. *The Evidence Continues to Grow*. National Committee for Citizens in Education, Columbia, Maryland, 1987.

LaForge, Ann E. *Eating: Win the Food Wars*. Pocket Books, New York, 1997.

———. *Tantrums: Secrets to Calming the Storm*. Pocket Books, New York, 1996.

Martin, Michael, Ph.D., NCSP, and Waltman-Greenwood, Cynthia, Ph.D., NCSP, editors. *Solve Your Child's School-Related Problems*. HarperCollins Publishers Inc., New York, 1995.

Miller, Mary Susan, Ph.D. *The School Book*. St. Martin's Press, New York, 1991.

Palfrey, Judith, M.D.; Schulman, Irving, M.D.; Katz, Samuel L., M.D.; and New, Maria I., M.D. *The Disney Encyclopedia of Baby and Child Care, volume 1, Infant and Child Development*. Hyperion, New York, 1995.

Perrone, Vito. *101 Educational Conversations to Have with Your Child* (series: Kindergarten Through Fifth Grade). Chelsea House Publishers, New York and Philadelphia, 1994.

Pulliam, John D., and Van Patten, James. *History of Education in America*, sixth edition. Prentice-Hall, Inc., Englewood Cliffs, New Jersey, 1995.

Rich, Dorothy, Ed.D. *MegaSkills*. Houghton-Mifflin Company, Boston, 1988.

———. *What Do We Say? What Do We Do?* Tom Doherty Associates, New York, 1997.

Schmitt, Barton, D., M.D., F.A.A.P. *Your Child's Health*. Bantam, New York, 1991.

Vander Zanden, James Wilfrid. *Human Development*, fifth edition. McGraw-Hill, Inc., New York, 1993.

Windell, James. *Children Who Say No When You Want Them to Say Yes*. Macmillan, New York, 1996.

ARTICLES

Atkins, Andrea. "Jumping Ahead, Staying Back." *Child*, February 1993.

Austin, Elizabeth. "Too Tired to Learn?" *Child,* June/July 1998.

Cushman, Kathleen. "What Kids Really Learn in Kindergarten." *Parents*, February 1995.

Denworth, Lydia. "Parents' 7 Biggest Questions about School." *Redbook*, September 1994.

Feder-Feitel, Lisa. "What's the Right Way to Teach Reading?" *Child*, November 1997.

Klein, Lee. "The Writing Process." *New York Family*, October 1997.

LaForge, Ann E. "After-School Activities: How Busy Should Your Child Be?" *Child*, May 1990.

———. "School's Out, Learning's In." *Child*, June/July 1990.

———. "Should You Help with Homework?" *Redbook*, September 1992.

———. "Raising a Child Who Loves to Read." *Redbook*, September 1993.

———. "Wooing a Reluctant Reader." *Redbook,* February 1994.

———. "How to Speak the New Math." *Redbook*, September 1994.

———. "What Really Happens to Your Child in School." *Redbook*, September 1995.

———. "Do You Praise Your Child Too Much?" *Redbook*, May 1996.

———. "7 Ways to Get Your Kids to Try Harder." *Redbook,* September 1996.

Lapinski, Susan. "Learning Disabilities: Mastering the Challenge." *Child*, November 1992.

Mason, Margaret. "Reading and Writing Activities in Elementary Grades." *Duke School for Children Newsletter*, November 1992.

———. "Developing Spelling Ability in the Elementary Grades." *Duke School for Children Newsletter*, January 1993.

Rich, Dorothy. "Activities to Strengthen Reading at

Home." *Instructor*, October 1988.

Throne, Jeanette, M.Ed. "Becoming a Kindergarten of Readers?" *Young Children*, September 1988.

BOOKLETS

Help Your Child Learn Math. National Council of Teachers of Mathematics, 1906 Association Drive, Reston, VA 22091.

Get Ready to Read! Tips for Parents of Young Children, You Can Help Your Child Connect Reading to Writing, Good Books Make Reading Fun for Your Child, Literacy Development and Early Childhood (Preschool through Grade 3). International Reading Association, 800 Barksdale Road, P.O. Box 8139, Newark, DE 19714.

Children's Writing: A Resource for Parents and Teachers. Northern Illinois Reading Council, 35 West 410 Crescent Drive, Dundee, IL 60118.